GOD'S PRIORITIES FOR TODAY'S WOMAN

Lisa Hughes

HARVEST HOUSE PUBLISHERS

EUGENE, OREGON

Cover by Dugan Design Group, Bloomington, Minnesota

Cover photo © I love images / Fotolia

Back cover author photo by Jason Dolbier

GOD'S PRIORITIES FOR TODAY'S WOMAN
Copyright © 2011 by Lisa Hughes
Published by Harvest House Publishers
Eugene, Oregon 97402
www.harvesthousepublishers.com

Library of Congress Cataloging-in-Publication Data
Hughes, Lisa, 1962-
God's priorities for today's woman / Lisa Hughes.
    p. cm.
ISBN 978-0-7369-3060-4 (pbk.)
1. Christian women—Religious life. I. Title.
BV4527.H8445 2011
248.8'43—dc22

2010028730

This book is dedicated to my husband, Jack, who the Lord has used as an instrument of grace and growth in my life, and to our children, Leah, Nate, and Mark, who bless me each and every day.

Acknowledgments

Writing a book is a monumental task, and though it begins as a solitary effort, the final product is very much the result of a team of people working to bring it to completion. The Lord graciously blessed me with just such a team who helped me in a variety of ways.

Without my husband Jack's encouragement I would never have dared embark on such a task and his prayers and strengthening from God's Word helped me to persevere through the long process. His insights and editing expertise were invaluable to me. Thank you for sacrificially serving me, dear!

My children encouraged me with e-mails and Scripture verses taped to the computer, and good-naturedly allowed me to use them as examples in this book. Thank you all!

I am so thankful for Steve Miller, my editor. Patience, encouragement, attention to detail, and a high view of God are the hallmarks of Steve's ministry to me. The Lord knows how often I thanked Him for Steve's wisdom and help. Steve, your help made this process a blessing. Thank you.

Thank you to my friends and family who faithfully prayed for me. How I have valued your prayers on my behalf.

Thanks to Karen Kelley for reading my manuscript and for being so encouraging to me!

Thanks too to Cristina Bolde, who provided an invaluable service when she applied her special test to the opening chapters of the book. Your help made a difference during the editing process.

I am also grateful to Barbara Barrick, who heard me teach on this material and encouraged me to put it into a book. The Lord used your words to confirm the desires of my own heart.

And above all, I am thankful to the Lord, for it is He who undergirded and guided the whole book-writing process. Each word is a testimony of the Lord's transforming work in me. It is with gratefulness that I can say He tested me chapter by chapter to see if I really believed and applied what I wrote. Thank you, dearest Lord, for the many kindnesses You showed me through this little journey.

Contents

An Invitation to Discovering God's Best for You

I remember as a young believer fearing that somehow I would miss knowing God's will for my life. It grieved me to think that I might miss it. For everything in me longed to please Him and do His will! Yet I was such a babe in Christ that I didn't know enough of the Bible to soothe my fearful thoughts. As I grew in my knowledge of God's Word, I came to realize that what God desires for us is much more accessible and easy to understand than I imagined.

Knowing God's will for our lives isn't like playing some shell game in which we sometimes happen upon what God wants us to do and other times we come up empty and lose out. Nor is it like archery, where we strive to hit the bull's eye of God's will but somehow can't seem to hit the mark. No, it's more like playing Candyland, a board game in which all the players win as long as they follow the path. God doesn't want us to "lose," and that's why He has plainly revealed His will within the pages of Scripture. And when it comes to grasping God's will, it helps to realize they are His *priorities* for our lives. God wants us to know the things that please Him. In fact, the Bible says that it's only when we follow His ways that we experience soul-satisfying comfort, peace, and hope.

Yet even when we have an ardent desire to please the Lord, we won't always find it easy to pursue His will. We may struggle at times to embrace His priorities for us. Sometimes our past experiences, our lack of biblical knowledge, our spiritual immaturity, or even our own sin can make it more difficult to obey the Lord. In spite of our wrestlings, we will desire His priorities to be our own, and our love for Him will win out over any objections we may have.

Longing to do our Father's will is a common attribute of *all* true believers. For that desire is born in us at the time of our conversion and grows throughout our lives here on earth. It's quite possible that's why you found yourself compelled to pick up this book—because you long to love, serve, and obey Him. You want to know what God's priorities are for your life, and you desire to live them out because doing so will bring true inner contentment and give people around you a glimpse of the wonderful ways He can work through us.

As you read along, you may feel left out of some of the priorities—you're not married, you don't have children, you live alone—and wonder if there's anything in these sections of the book for you. There is! *Every* priority can be applied in *some* way by *every* woman. God hasn't made any mistakes regarding your life or His will as recorded in the Scriptures. *These priorities are for you!*

The degree to which you apply each priority in your life may change over time as your circumstances change. Yet your commitment to them need never change. You may find yourself single, childless, or still living at home with your parents, yet each priority is designed by God for your benefit. God's Word is all-encompassing and has something in it for everyone—and that includes you at *any* stage of your life.

Let the words from the hymn below reside as a prayer in your heart while you read in the pages to come about God's priorities. And then may that prayer rise as an anthem of your commitment to God's will for your life as you live your life *all for Jesus*!

All for Jesus, all for Jesus
All my being's ransomed pow'rs:
All my tho'ts and words and doings,
All my days and all my hours.

Let my hands perform His bidding,
Let my feet run in His ways;
Let my eyes see Jesus only,
Let my lips speak forth His praise.[1]

Part 1

The Call to Follow God's Priorities

Chapter 1

God's Unchanging Priorities for You

It happened again. Our family was watching reruns of the TV show *Murder, She Wrote,* which aired on television from 1984 to 1995, when the fabled "generation gap" reared its head and roared, making its presence known in our living room. This time that roaring generation gap was incarnated in the form of our three teenagers hooting at some of the hairstyles and clothes worn by the stars in the TV series. I energetically defended the "big" hair and large shoulder pads in the outfits because I too had aspired to big hair in the 1980s. This only served to make my kids laugh even more. Apparently exclaiming, "Everyone wore their hair like that," and "That was considered really fashionable at the time" didn't convince my teenaged jury that those styles were really "cool," for their own sense of fashion and beauty has been defined by the time in which they live.

Looking back, I do have to admit some of those hairstyles and clothing fashions were funny looking! It reminded me once again of the transitory nature of what we consider "in" or even what we consider beautiful. While it's always hard to predict what may start a beauty or fashion trend, it's easy to predict that whatever or whoever starts the trend affects society in a powerful way. No wonder the beauty and fashion industries spend millions of dollars on advertising alone! If they can spark a trend, then a whole generation will be shaped by it—to the point that multitudes of women will happily grace the streets attired in leg warmers, permed hair, and blue eye shadow.

God's Standard for Beauty Does Not Change

Not only does the world's criteria for *external* beauty change, but its standard for what constitutes beautiful character or a fulfilling life changes too. And it changes constantly! What's in one season is out the next. It's a challenge to keep up with it all. As we look around us it's obvious that Satan, the god of this world (2 Corinthians 4:4), desires to twist and subvert God's plans in any way he can. Through Satan's influence and man's own sinfulness, the world is convinced that what is new or different is always best, and that God's ways are outdated.

The world would have us believe that God's ways cannot exist in today's culture, that they are unnecessary and outlandishly archaic. Yet God's priorities for women are neither outdated nor irrelevant. God's purposes for us were created out of His wisdom and love. They are perfect and are just right for us no matter who we are or what circumstances we face.

And though the world may shift and morph, there is one place we can turn to where the standard remains the same, and that's the Word of God. Our God's unchanging character and purposes are completely preserved within the pages of Scripture. And because God is perfect in everything He does, then what He deems good and right—even beautiful—is the true standard, no matter what comes and goes in our ever-changing world. When we understand God's plan for womanhood, it helps us cultivate proper attitudes about being a woman and how to live out the roles of wife, mother, and homemaker. And one of the best places to study those priorities is in the book of Titus.

God's Priorities Revealed

Within the space of three verses, Titus chapter 2 provides a succinct definition of a woman's role and calling. The passage reveals God's priorities for women and the high standard of godly character *all* women are to embody—at every age and in every life situation. This information is narrowed down to the essentials and allows us to zero in on exactly what God desires for us as women. And that's good news for us because Titus 2:3-5 provides a practical and straightforward look into what God deems important for every woman.

Understanding the Background of the Book of Titus

Have you ever interacted with someone and became somewhat irritated or even appalled by their behavior, only to discover later some extenuating circumstances that explained their strange actions? It's so helpful to know those things! A little bit of background information can make such a difference in how we respond to a person, and *it is no different when we study the Bible.* When we understand the background of the apostle Paul's letter to Titus, we will appreciate all the more the significance of the instructions given to women in chapter 2.

The Conditions at Crete

In this letter the apostle Paul counsels his friend and co-worker in the faith, Titus, who had previously traveled with Paul on some missionary journeys. The Scriptures reveal Titus to be a man eager to jump in where needed, a man who wasn't afraid to work hard and didn't bend to peer pressure. Those were the perfect qualities for a man left alone on the island of Crete and charged with overseeing the growth of multiple churches. It couldn't have been easy for Titus to minister on Crete, for the Cretans were proud of their sin. In his letter to Titus, Paul even quoted a common saying they had about themselves: "Cretans are always liars, evil beasts, lazy gluttons" (Titus 1:12). The Cretans reveled in their hard-heartedness, yet it was among these people that the gospel had made an inroad and lives had been transformed.

The Charge to Titus

And it was Titus's job on Crete to oversee these new believers and to train leaders in the fledgling churches. Wherever truth blossoms, false religions attempt to plant their noxious weeds of heretical teaching nearby, and Crete was no exception. Paul explained the psyche of the false teachers when he stated, "They profess to know God, but by their deeds they deny Him, being detestable and disobedient and worthless for any good deed" (Titus 1:12).

In contrast to the false teachers' impure and greedy behavior and heretical teaching, Paul reminded Titus of his calling and his priorities as a pastor. Most likely Titus could hear Paul's voice ring in his ears as he read from Paul's letter, "But as for you, speak the things which are fitting for sound doctrine" (2:1). This was Titus's primary duty—to continuously preach and teach God's Word to the people, which would then equip them and help them to grow in the faith. Like lights on a runway which guide a plane to safety, so Titus 2:1 guides us toward the information that provides us with purpose, hope, and peace. What we read in Titus 2:1 shows us how valuable the details in the rest of the chapter are. Let's look together and see what verse 1 has to say to you and me.

The First Bookend of Titus 2

Every book lover knows the value of bookends. We have quite a few that grace the bookshelves in our living room, and I love finding new bookends that add grace and flair. Yet whether the bookends are nondescript pieces of aluminum or artistic sculptures, every one of them is designed for the same simple function: to showcase the books on the shelves. A bookend can have artistic and decorative merit, but it exists to display and support the books. And God has placed two wonderfully instructive bookends in Titus chapter 2 whose purpose is to *reveal the value* of the verses in between them. So let's examine both bookends, starting with the first one, which is Titus 2:1. What we learn from looking at its fine details will *prepare* our hearts for the priorities God has placed on the shelf.

Why Being Proper Is Important for You

Titus is exhorted to continuously teach the things *fitting* for every believer. Fitting—now *there's* a word we don't often hear these days. The word seems to belong to a different time and place, to a world in which people responded to "doing one's duty" and "doing what's right." Because it's not a commonly used term anymore, we need to pay careful attention to the word's meaning, for it alerts us to the great value of what is about to follow.

History reveals that codes of conduct and the sense of what is suitable continues to change. In fact it seems that the world's goal is to keep changing whatever is viewed as fitting or right. But God never changes and His standard for suitable, proper, and fitting behavior for every believer remains the same. For example, in Ephesians 5:3-4 we read, "Immorality or any impurity or greed must not even be named among you, as is *proper* among saints; and there must be no filthiness and silly talk, or coarse jesting, which are not *fitting*, but rather giving of thanks." In those verses we learn what God considers appropriate behavior for believers.

So when we read in Titus 2:1 that Titus is to speak fitting, appropriate, and proper words that go along with sound doctrine, it decisively proclaims what God wants every believer to know about acting properly. Our goal as Christian women is to understand what is proper for us, and then to live it out because we love the Lord. The good news is we don't have to guess what things God considers fitting for Christian women because He lets us know in His Word!

Why Learning What Is Sound Is Important for You

When Titus was told to continuously teach the things proper and appropriate for believers to know, that meant he was to teach sound doctrine. A veterinarian might say, after examining a horse, that his legs are *sound*, or healthy. They aren't crippled or deficient in some way, but strong and whole. So when we hear the term sound doctrine, we can think of doctrine that is healthy, whole, and complete.

The physical fitness industry makes a mint off people's desire to be fit and healthy. No one wants to feel weak or physically unhealthy. And when it comes to our *spiritual fitness,* we should show even more concern about what's good for us. Thankfully, God hasn't left it up to us to figure out what things make for whole and healthy Christian living. Verses 2-10 of Titus chapter 2 reveal what we need to know, understand, and apply to our lives if we want to become spiritually fit.

Why Sound Doctrine Is Important for You

Everything that Paul tells Titus to teach the believers in Titus 2:2-10 matches up with sound doctrine. These characteristics complement the doctrines of God. In essence, sound doctrine holds hands with the priorities listed in verses 2-10.

You may be saying, "Sound doctrine? *Doctrine?* What is that? It sounds boring and a little scary." But let me put your mind at ease. Doctrine is simply the collected instruction of the Bible designed to produce spiritual maturity and Christlikeness. Doctrine helps us become spiritually healthy. And we *all* need doctrine so we can grow more like Jesus.

Paul explains in 1 Timothy 4:6 that sound doctrine is something we nourish our souls with and then teach to others. When we feed upon the healthy doctrines of God's Word, we grow spiritually strong, which actually sounds quite helpful and interesting!

Sound doctrine is for everyone. That's why almost every people group that can be found in a church is addressed in Titus 2: older men, older women, young women, young men (including Titus), and even bondslaves. Paul even included himself in the closing verses. *No one* is left out. *Everyone* must receive counsel and instruction about how to grow in godliness, and that comes from sound doctrine.

The Second Bookend of Titus 2

With the first bookend in place, we can now turn our attention to the second bookend, which will help us gain a clearer understanding of God's priorities. This bookend is found at the end of the chapter, in verse 15. Paul wrote, "These things speak and exhort and reprove with all authority. Let no one disregard you." You might be thinking, *Wow! That sounds serious.* You're right, it *is* important. Commands like that are sure to capture anyone's attention, and they were designed to capture ours!

Why "These Things" Are Important for You

So what was so important about "these things" that Paul wanted Titus to be sure to speak? Paul was referring to all the priorities and commands of verses 2-10, the godly priorities God has made known to all the members of the church. Every little detail and comment about older and younger men, older and younger women, and slaves is summed up in the two words "these things."

With phrases like "speak and exhort and reprove," "with all

authority," and "let no one disregard you," even if we are experiencing brain fog we can still figure out that whatever comes in between those bookends is not merely optional for us. *The information sandwiched between those "verse bookends" contains God's will for us.* The bookend verses of Titus 2:1 and 2:15 not only showcase God's priorities for us, they actually insist we listen to and heed them.

Why Regarding God's Word Is Important for You

Titus 2:15, our second bookend, closes with the command to Titus, "Let no one disregard you." Now that's a tall order! Bible teacher John MacArthur stated that a pastor "has spiritual authority only to the extent that what he says conforms to God's Word."[1] So if a pastor is carefully and faithfully teaching God's Word to us, and he gets to a section of Scripture that we would rather not hear, how should we respond? Titus 2:15 tells us: God's Word is not to be disregarded.

We need to remember that the preaching of God's Word is one of the means God has given to aid us in our spiritual growth, so whether we are hearing it taught or reading it ourselves, we mustn't discount or trivialize His Word. Instead, we are to *really* listen to it and heed it. Everything we need to know for living the Christian life is contained in the pages of the Bible, and for us women, specific information about God's priorities for us is detailed in Titus 2:3-5.

A SELECTIVE RESPONSE

Our middle child, Nate, was generally obedient and cheerful as he was growing up. But when he was little, if I called him to come to the dinner table while he was engrossed with his Legos, he wouldn't respond! He wouldn't even acknowledge he had heard my voice. I naively began to wonder if he had a hearing problem. But my wise husband devised a plan to test my theory.

One day when Nate was again playing with his toys, my husband had me call Nate to the table for dinner. No response, no turn of the head, nothing to indicate he heard me call him. Then my husband whispered one word in my ear: "Cookie." Instantly, Nate perked up and popped into the kitchen looking for the cookies. I'd been had! But that little story illustrates what Paul is conveying to Titus: "Don't let anyone disregard God's Word. The things you are communicating to them are too important, too valuable for them to ignore."

> If we desire to know God's will for our lives, then we need to heed the Scriptures. God's Word, after all, is God's will!

A WHOLEHEARTED RESPONSE

We must eagerly value *all* of God's Word and respond enthusiastically to all of it, not just select portions of it. When we have regard for something, we esteem it and pay attention to it. And just like our son Nate had to learn to regard my voice, whether the words *cookie* or *clean your room* were on my lips, so must we learn to regard God's Word whenever we read it or hear it proclaimed because it is *God's Word*.

Because Titus was teaching God's Word, he was to make sure the people tuned in and listened. God had commanded it and communicated it for the blessing and benefit of His children, and He wanted His children to regard it as great treasure. This is true for us too. If we desire to know God's will for our lives, then we need to heed the Scriptures. God's Word, after all, is God's will!

What the Bookends Tell You About God's Priorities

Now you see the purpose of our little background lesson about the bookends of Titus 2:1 and 2:15. These bookends showcase the priorities of Titus 2:3-5 and reveal how highly God values them. The first bookend says, "As for you, speak the things which are fitting for sound doctrine" (verse 1). The second bookend says, "These things speak and exhort and reprove with all authority. Let no one disregard you" (verse 15). We see that all the instructions *between* the bookends are of utmost importance.

Even before we begin our tour of God's unchanging priorities for women in the upcoming chapters, the bookends help us understand the supreme place priorities *must* have in our lives. And that's probably why you're reading this book. You want to know what God's priorities are for your life, and you want to live in such a way that you can effectively apply them.

God's Unchanging Priorities and You

God values the contents of Titus 2:3-5 to the point that He wants us to make sure that we hear it, regard it, and put it into action in our lives. These are God's priorities for us! And that's important information we don't want to miss. Yet frequently people dismiss the Bible's commands as being old-fashioned and irrelevant for today. And many women would like to believe God would change His mind if He really knew and understood our modern culture and their personal situations. Yet God truly does know the issues we face. He didn't make any mistakes giving us His Word exactly as we have it in our Bibles today. God knew *precisely* what He wanted to communicate for all time, *for our time*, and it is recorded in Titus 2:3-5.

Choosing to Do What God Wants

If we discount God's Word and refuse to apply it to our lives, we aren't rejecting the apostle Paul or even our pastor or Sunday school teacher. We are actually rejecting God Himself (1 Thessalonians 4:8). Too often believers act as if living the Christian life is like joining a health club where members can pick and choose whatever exercise machines and fitness classes are appealing to them. *They* choose the fitness activities they want to engage in, while the fitness center serves *them*. Many believers apply that kind of mentality to the Christian life today. The emphasis is upon what *they* want to do, how *they* want to live, and how *they* want to implement God's Word in their lives, rather than what *God* wants them to do, how *God* wants them to live, and how *God* wants them to implement His Word in their lives.

God called you to follow Him. He made this possible by sending His Son to die on the cross for your sins. If Christ has redeemed you from sin and death, then you owe Him a debt of love and gratitude. And it is that debt of love and gratitude that causes us to love what He loves and make His priorities our priorities.

Seeking God's Best for Your Life

Sometimes we make foolish, uninformed, or even selfish choices. It would be nice if we always knew the best thing for us to do. But we don't always know that. Yet the Lord does—He *always* knows what's best for us. And His best for us has been preserved in Titus 2:3-5. We don't need to try to figure out what's important to God; He's told us exactly what He considers important for Christian women. And that's the Titus 2:3-5 priorities He has for every one of His daughters.

Titus 2:3-5 isn't a take-it-or-leave-it passage. Within these verses are the unchanging priorities of God's heart for you, for me, and for every woman so we can live lives that are pleasing to Him. Knowing that, we must ask ourselves these questions: How do I *regard* God's priorities found in Titus 2:3-5? And how can I take these priorities to heart and *apply* them?

This is our opportunity to grasp these priorities with delight and trust, and seek to live them out for God's glory. Let's discover together what God desires for us!

We need to understand God's plan for womanhood so we can cultivate proper attitudes toward all that He has called us to do. Titus 2:3-5 is not the only place we read about God's priorities for women, but within those three verses we find a concise and succinct definition of a woman's role and calling. The passage reveals the high standard of godly character all women are to embody, while addressing the priorities and ministries of women, whether in youth or old age. These verses are extremely practical and straightforward, leaving a well-marked path for us to follow.

Let's begin our study with a quick look at the structure and background of the book. It is important we take the time to do this because it will help us understand Titus 2:3-5 better.

1. Who is the author? What details do you learn about that author from the book of Titus?

2. To whom is the book written? What details do you learn about the recipients within the three chapters of Titus?

3. In a few sentences summarize the contents of chapter 1. As you write, imagine trying to explain what chapter 1 is about to a fourth grader.

Now summarize the contents of chapter 2.

Finally, summarize the contents of chapter 3.

4. What is the apostle Paul's purpose in writing the book? Cite the chapter and verse where you found your answer.

5. Following an author's train of thought from one chapter to another is an important Bible study technique, so let's put this rule of Bible study into practice: Explain how chapter 1 leads into our passage of Titus 2:3-5.

6. What do the verses immediately before and after Titus 2:3-5 talk about? How are they all related in subject?

7. Is Paul making suggestions for Christian character here, or are these commands to be obeyed? For a hint, read verse 15.

8. This isn't a take-it-or-leave-it passage. This is God's plan for the church, and His priorities for women. In what ways are you making it your business to "excel still more" in these areas?

Chapter 2

"The" Mindset
for Every Woman

I never realized one little piece of plastic could make such a difference when it came to fixing broken refrigerators. Jack and I were newlyweds living in an old apartment built on one of the oldest streets in Boise, Idaho, and in that old dwelling was an old refrigerator we inherited from the previous tenants when we moved in.

One morning we opened the freezer portion of the fridge to discover that it was completely frosted over. My Mr. Fix-it husband sprang into action. After an initial inspection, he surmised that the freezer fan was broken and needed replacing. Soon he had different pieces and parts of the refrigerator removed so he could take out the freezer fan and replace it, but to his surprise he discovered that the freezer fan worked fine. Nothing was wrong with it. Hmmm—that meant a more complex problem to solve. So he continued testing the handful of other parts of the refrigerator, only to discover that they too were functioning properly.

After watching my husband try to solve The Mystery of the Frosty Freezer for over an hour, I happened to remember a little incident that had occurred the previous day when I was putting away some groceries in the freezer. Unsure if the information was pertinent or not, I casually mentioned it to him.

"Sweety," I said, "I don't know if this makes a difference, but there was a little black dealy-bob that fell out of the freezer when I opened it up yesterday. Would that have anything to do with our problem?"

I showed him the black dealy-bob that I had carefully set aside on the windowsill, just in case it was important. Imagine my surprise when my fix-it husband looked at it, opened the freezer door, stuck it in a hole that looked like it was designed for just such an object, pushed it into place, and wah-la! The freezer fan began to run again!

"Honey bunches," he began in Newlywed Speak, "why didn't you tell me about the black dealy-bob earlier? I could have fixed the freezer in one minute instead of spending an hour on it."

"I'm so sorry, lovey-doo. I didn't think it was important," I replied.

That was the day I learned that even seemingly insignificant pieces of information can make a world of difference when it comes to fixing things around the house. Who would have thought that one little piece of plastic could make such a difference to an entire refrigerator? Obviously, not me! Even now, whenever anything breaks around the house I try to convey—complete with sound effects—every significant and often insignificant detail that may prove helpful for its eventual repair.

In a similar manner, there is one word nestled in the midst of the instructions for women in Titus 2:3-5 that we can easily overlook. Just like my little black dealy-bob, this one word may not attract our attention at first, but upon closer inspection we gain insight into its value. This word grows richer in meaning as we study it and see how it is used to focus our attention on God's priorities for women.

We have already studied how the bookends of Titus 2:1 and 2:15 reveal the importance of the priorities sandwiched between them. We looked at the admonitions to Titus to continually speak the things that go along with sound doctrine and preach God's Word with all authority, and the high value of God's Word, which we must apply to our lives. Now we turn our attention to the one all-important word that provides *the* mindset we need to have as we learn about God's priorities for women.

Usually when I study and teach through a passage I start at the beginning of the text and explain what it means step by step. However, when I studied this passage I discovered one word in the middle of it that changed my usual approach. This passage has one key word that influences the priorities contained in Titus 2:3-5. It reveals to us the mindset every woman is to have about God's priorities for her. We find that word in verse 4, which states the older women are to "encourage" the younger women in a variety of ways. The word "encourage" is the hinge on which the whole text moves.

Read Titus 2:3-5 in its entirety and pay special attention to the word "encourage" in the middle of our priorities:

> Older women likewise are to be reverent in their behavior, not malicious gossips nor enslaved to much wine, teaching what is good, so that they may encourage the young women to love their husbands, to love their children, to be sensible, pure, workers at home, kind, being subject to their own husbands, so that the word of God will not be dishonored.

The word "encourage" is rich with meaning and the ways it is translated in different modern Bible translations shows this. The New American Standard version of Titus 2:4 urges the older women to "*encourage the young women.*" The King James Version says older women are to "*teach* the young women to be sober." The New International Version and the English Standard Version both use the word "train" instead of "encourage" or "teach." Each of these translations provides insight into this particular word's meaning that older women are to encourage, teach, and train younger women.

The word used in the original Greek text means "to cause to be of sound mind, to restore to one's senses, to bring someone to reason or duty."[1] It is translated "sensible" or "sensibly" in verses 2, 5, 6, and 12 in the New American Standard Bible. All of this teaches us that the older women are to train and restore the young women to their senses, helping them to be sober-minded in their duties as wives, mothers, and keepers of the home.

What this means for us today is exactly what it meant for the first-century women on the island of Crete. Women must be trained, focused, and sober-minded about the priorities revealed to them in Titus 2:3-5. This is *the* mindset that is to govern and guide our lives as Christian women.

Paul urges Timothy to have the same emphasis on sober-mindedness toward his ministry in 2 Timothy 4:5, where he says, "But you, be sober in all things, endure hardship, do the work of an evangelist, fulfill your ministry." *Oh dear*, you may be thinking, *that sounds dreadfully boring. I suppose that means never being able to smile or have fun. Words like* sober *and* endure *spell D-R-U-D-G-E-R-Y.*

Never fear, dearheart. Drudgery is *not* what God wants for us. Believers are to live a life of love for God, and that can never be boring! Second Corinthians 5:14-15 says, "*The love of Christ controls us*, having concluded this, that one died for all, therefore all died; and He died for all, so that they who live might no longer live for themselves, but for Him who died and rose again on their behalf." Understanding Christ's great sacrifice on our behalf compels and constrains us to live for Him, so that every duty, which previously seemed tedious, is transformed into an opportunity to show our gratitude and love to our Savior.

So when it comes to being sober-minded about our priorities, we don't find it difficult or cumbersome because we are motivated by Christ's love for us and our love for Him. To be sober-minded is to mentally snap to attention, straighten the shoulders, and prepare for action. It rules out a reluctant, halfhearted "nose to the grindstone" attitude toward God's priorities for us. Words like *serious, reasonable, careful, wise, disciplined*, and *self-controlled* describe what it means to be sober-minded.[2] All these words reveal the mindset we need to have toward God's priorities.

Biblical Reasons to Be Sober-minded

When we are serious about something it is because we understand its worth, and what could be more valuable than God's priorities found in Titus 2:3-5? Don't you think they are worth some serious consideration and careful thought? I know I do! Let's look at some of the reasons the Bible gives us for being sober-minded about the things of God.

We Need to Make the Most of Opportunity

First Thessalonians 5:4-6 reminds us to wisely use the time we have on this earth, and be alert and sober rather than wasting the opportunities we have. Paul wrote in verse 8, "Since we are of the day, let us be sober, having put on the breastplate of faith and love, and as a helmet, the hope of salvation." If you are a believer, you are "of the day."

Another way of saying we are of the day is to say that believers walk in the light because God is light (1 John 1:5-7). Everyone knows each day only has a certain number of daylight hours, so it is essential that we take advantage of the light while it is available.

I have a friend who is a missionary in Malawi. During the first year she and her family lived there, they discovered that the house water was shut off four to five days a week between 7:00 a.m. to 4:00 p.m. During that year, water deprivation made her sober-minded about getting her chores done. She learned to make the most of those hours when the water was on by bathing her children, doing the dishes, preparing food, and doing the laundry. Knowing the water would soon be turned off motivated her to work quickly, efficiently, and purposefully. And that is exactly the attitude God desires us to have about our priorities.

A sober-minded woman makes the most of her opportunities.

We Need to Remember Time Is Short

The apostle Peter liked the word *sober* and used it three times in the book of 1 Peter. He urged, "Therefore, prepare your minds for action, keep sober in spirit, fix your hope completely on the grace to be brought to you at the revelation of Jesus Christ" (1:13). "Prepare your minds," "keep sober in spirit," and "fix your hope." That is exactly what Dorothy portrayed in the movie *The Wizard of Oz* when she said, "There's no place like home." Our focus is not on our earthly home, but on our home in heaven, where we will see Jesus. It is wise to regularly remind ourselves, "This world is not my home. This world is not my home." As we do so, we maintain a proper perspective on the world's passing allurements and remember that soon we will live in heaven and see our Savior face to face!

Peter reiterated the same idea when he reminded us, "The end of all things is near; therefore, be of sound judgment and sober spirit for the purpose of prayer" (1 Peter 4:7). Again we see that the shortness of time, "the end of all things is near," is a powerful motivation toward sober-minded living. In fact, the brevity of life and our consideration of it should move us to pray fervently and faithfully during the time we have left on this earth.

Knowing I don't have much time to accomplish something helps me to hop to it and get things done. Suddenly the extraneous things are not as important. Instead, only the priorities need my attention. If we have plans for guests to come over, I may start with grandiose ideas of how clean I want everything to be and how elaborate a dinner I want to prepare. But in the end, if time is short, my goal is to accomplish the priority—dinner! If anything more gets done, it is icing on the cake. Knowing time is short helps us to focus on our priorities, like the ones clearly revealed in Titus 2:3-5.

A sober-minded woman remembers time is short.

We Need to Remain Vigilant

Peter alerts us to the fact that Satan "prowls around like a roaring lion, seeking someone to devour" (1 Peter 5:8). You are that someone! While in South Africa preaching at some conferences, my husband had the opportunity to tour a wild animal park. While on the tour, in the safety of a well-fortified Land Rover, the group drove by a small band of tourists out of their vehicle, cheerfully standing by a sign that warned, "Do Not Get Out of Your Vehicle!" The guide grimly related that every year tourists flippantly disregard the warnings, get out of their cars to take pictures, and are attacked and eaten by lions, cheetahs, or leopards. Understanding there is a lion stalking us should cause us to proceed with caution.

When Peter says Satan "prowls around like a *roaring* lion," he means that Satan is hungry to devour us and ready to attack. Soldiers maintain vigilance when they know any enemy is approaching. As Christians, we cannot afford to downplay the danger we are in knowing that our enemy, Satan, is seeking to devour us.

When we consider the state of our world, it becomes obvious there is a great need for women to remain sober-minded about God's priorities for them. Satan is attacking the church and God's Word at every turn. He uses the world and its many distractions, pleasures, and false religions to devour the weak in faith. Christian families are falling apart. Many young women have no idea how to take care of a home and family because they never had a mother who was in the home to teach them. When women don't adhere to God's priorities they become like wounded wildebeests on the African plain—easy targets for the roaring lion. Therefore, women need to be alert and sober-minded about God's priorities for them. Without careful vigilance we become like foolish tourists in the game parks of Satan's domain.

A sober-minded woman is alert to Satan's wiles.

We need to make the most of the opportunities God has given us, remember that our time here on earth is short, and never forget that our enemy, Satan, prowls about seeking to devour us as we focus our attention on God's priorities. These are all excellent reasons why we need to have the mindset of being serious about God's plan for us found in Titus 2:3-5.

A Picture of Sober-mindedness

You might be thinking, *Okay, I can see from the Bible that I need to be sober-minded about God's priorities, but what is it going to look like in my life? I don't want to become a sourpuss who never cracks a smile.* I understand your concerns! I wouldn't want to live like that either. Thankfully, God provides us with many texts in His Word which, like pieces of a puzzle, we can assemble to form a clear picture of the attitudes and actions of the serious-minded believer. You'll see that we can have a sober-minded attitude about God's priorities and still be happy and fun to be around!

Accurate Thinking

When Paul discussed the various kinds of spiritual gifts that are given to every believer at salvation, he stated, "I say to everyone among you not to think more highly of himself than he ought to think; but to think so as *to have sound judgment*, as God has allotted to each a measure of faith" (Romans 12:3). This means every believer has been given one or more spiritual gifts to benefit the body of Christ, and every gift is essential to the proper working of the church. In essence, Paul was saying, "Don't think your gift is too insignificant to be used by God, and on the other hand, don't think too highly of the gifts you have because it is a gift of God. Not one of us has earned or deserved our gift." A sober-minded focus upon God's Word helps us to see ourselves accurately in light of the Scriptures, which ultimately allows us to relax and enjoy our position in the body of Christ.

> When our eyes stay on Him we maintain the
> mindset we need to have and won't find ourselves
> distracted from our God-given priorities.

A Good Steward of Time

As we learned earlier from 1 Thessalonians 5:8, we show we are serious about the things of God when we pursue growth in godliness and avoid idling away our days. This is exactly what Moses had in mind in Psalm 90:12: "So teach us to number our days, that we may present to You a heart of wisdom." We exhibit a cheerful, sober-minded spirit when we are faithful to attend to our daily tasks and seek the Lord. When our eyes stay on Him we maintain the mindset we need to have and won't find ourselves distracted from our God-given priorities.

Emulate the Proverbs 31 Woman

The Proverbs 31 woman was a good steward of her time and more. The deeds extolled about her reveal careful thought, wise judgment, and a sincere delight in blessing her family and honoring the Lord. She was sober-minded about her priorities.

- She was wise toward her husband and thought of ways to bless him (verse 11).
- She did him good and not evil all the days of her life (verse 12).
- She worked willingly and cheerfully for her family's sake (verse 13).
- She saw value in hard work, especially when she saw the fruit of her labors (verse 18).

- She planned ahead for the needs of her family (verses 20-21).

- Her life was one of wisdom, careful thought, and trust in the Lord, which enabled her to smile at the future (verse 25).

- She understood the value of kind and wise speech (verse 26).

- Her prudent judgment motivated her faithful care of her home (verse 27).

- She did not give in to idleness (verse 27).

- And finally, her family understood that her patient industry and diligent efforts were rooted in her love for the Lord (verses 28-31).

To become a Proverbs 31 woman we must develop and maintain a serious mindset toward the priorities God has for us. Having this focus shows our regard for God's Word. We must respond with a whole-hearted, "Yes! I want to concentrate on Your priorities so I can honor You, Lord."

Building a Biblical Thought Foundation

When it comes to the mindset we should have about our priorities as listed in Titus 2:3-5, we can't act like foolish tourists who ignore the warning signs in the animal park and treat God's Word with flippant disregard. Rather, we must recognize the wisdom of God at work. He knows what is best when it comes to the roles and duties He has given to every Christian woman. Oh, let us be like wise tourists who heed God's Word and delight in obeying Him! Learning to obey God's Word and love His ways comes from thinking biblically.

What You Think Paves the Way for How You Live

Our youngest son, Mark, plays the piano. There are times when, while learning a new piece of music, his fingers have trouble playing the notes his eyes read on the page. He has learned that if he practices and practices but can't seem to make progress, it is best to take a break. When he comes back to the piano the next day, the trouble spot is often more easily overcome. The mind, dwelling on these things, paves the way for the actions. That illustrates well the reason we have spent some significant time laying the foundation for Titus 2:3-5. Your understanding of just how important God's priorities are and your willingness to maintain that mindset will help you to more easily make those priorities real in your life.

> The key to success and fulfillment in every
> aspect of our lives lies in the Word of God.

Acquire Wisdom from God's Word

As always for a Christian, the key to success and fulfillment in every aspect of our lives lies in the Word of God. And cultivating a prudent and sensible mindset about our priorities is no exception. Proverbs 18:15 states, "The mind of the prudent acquires knowledge, and the ear of the wise seeks knowledge." A Titus 2 woman recognizes her need for training and instruction in God's priorities.

Every believer must learn to feed upon God's wisdom, and that can only be found in God's Word. Proverbs 2:6-7 states, "The LORD gives wisdom; from His mouth come knowledge and understanding. He stores up sound wisdom for the upright; He is a shield to those who walk in integrity." The Lord is the very source of wisdom, and He stores up wisdom for believers. But wisdom stored and not used is merely head knowledge, which is why the Lord also helps believers apply godly wisdom to their lives. His wisdom is a protection for us and guards us from sin and folly. What a blessing it is to have that shield in our lives!

Another reason for acquiring wisdom from God's Word is found in Psalm 37:31: "The law of his God is in his heart; his steps do not slip." With God's Word stored securely in our hearts we will not slip into sin or fall prey to Satan's attacks. It is the heart of all sensible, sober-minded living.

You can put a biblical thought foundation into place in your life simply by reading your Bible daily. A great way to build this discipline is to follow a Bible-reading plan that will help you read through the entire Bible in a year. Or you might want to try choosing a specific book of the Bible to read, and then read it every day for a month. If it's a long book, divide it into sections and read the first section every day for a month, then move on to the second section and read it for a month, and so on. As you read each day, keep track of what you observe about the book. Look for the main theme of the book, how it is put together, the repeated subjects, any commands that are given and why, and what you learn about God's character. This will help you pull together and systematize what you have learned through your reading.

Another way to store God's Word in your heart and grow in biblical wisdom is to do a Bible study on a topic or issue you are struggling with, a matter you've always been interested in, or a subject that will aid you in some way with your spiritual growth. For example, you may want to study the "do not fret" and "do not be anxious" passages of the Bible if you are struggling with anxiety. With the help of a concordance, you will want to look up every passage in the Bible that talks about that topic, then note how each verse is used in the passage. Be sure to pay attention to the context of the verse. Understanding how that particular verse fits in with the surrounding verses will help you gain insight about overcoming anxiety, or whatever topic it is you've chosen to study.

Then observe who is not to be anxious, the ways to overcome anxiety, and what truths you can learn about God. There are some great software programs and online resources that will help you do this.[3] After studying each passage, summarize what you have learned. Try putting what you have learned onto a prayer list, and ask God to help you apply those truths. You can even try memorizing the key Bible verses that help instruct and encourage you.

Another great way to glean biblical wisdom is by reading one chapter from the book of Proverbs every day for a month. Because there are 31 chapters in the book, you will finish Proverbs in a month. Keep a record of what you learn about the different types of people described in the book of Proverbs: the fool, the righteous person, the scoffer, and the boisterous woman. Then summarize what you learn about each person and what he or she does. The book of Proverbs is a treasure trove of wisdom for issues related to the tongue, parenting, marriage, diligence, and more.

Finally, memorize God's Word. I know, I know…nobody wants to do this, but Bible memorization is crucial to thinking biblically. Everyone can memorize! We regularly memorize large chunks of the Bible during the course of our ladies' Bible study each year. And we have women in their eighties and nineties who are still hiding God's Word in their hearts. It's never too late to begin implementing this important discipline, though I must prepare you: It does take time and commitment on your part.

If you aren't in the habit of memorizing Scripture, begin today by committing Titus 2:3-5 to memory. Simply read it ten times slowly. Say it aloud. Think about it as you read. Pray through it, asking God to help you understand and apply each part. Soon it will guide your thinking and aid you in decision making, and with God's Word as your guide you will be on your way to living out God's priorities in your life. Let's get started!

Our Earnest Duty

We are to undertake God's priorities from Titus 2:3-5 with sober-minded consideration. God is serious about these priorities, and He wants us to be as well! They are *our* priorities. They are our responsibility, and we are to make an effort to engage in them with excellence.

The information found in these verses isn't like the food found in a buffet-style restaurant, where you can choose to eat whatever looks good to you. Instead, the information given here is like the food given to you at home as a kid—whatever Mom cooked and put on the table was what you had to eat. The Titus 2:3-5 priorities are what God has dished up and put on the table for your good. And because God has placed them on *your* plate, it's time to dig in with gusto to His life-nourishing priorities.

The Benefits of Living Out God's Priorities

God greatly values the priorities of Titus 2:3-5, and that is why He desires us to maintain a sober-minded attitude about them. Just think about what your life would look like if you embraced these priorities with the mindset God emphasizes in these verses. Even if you have already committed yourself to living according to Titus 2:3-5, we all have areas in which there is room to grow. Can you think of any of the Titus 2:3-5 priorities that need focused attention? I know I always have *something* in my life that needs work. Let God shine the light of His Word on the priorities you need to improve upon as we continue to study them together. With the clear instructions given in Titus 2:3-5, there is no more guesswork. No more wondering if you are on track. God has made His will for you clear in His Word.

There are questions you must ask yourself. "Am I applying these priorities with the focus and diligence God desires of me?" And, "Am I maintaining a proper mindset toward God's priorities?" Even if fulfilling some of these priorities is a stretch for you and you find it difficult to comply with them, that doesn't let you off the hook.

God makes no mistakes. You must make His instructions in Titus 2:3-5 a priority in your life. You will find some of God's priorities a pure joy to apply, and you will find others more difficult to obey. Even then, God will use them for your good. The struggles and difficulties you may undergo will cause you to cling more closely to the Lord. Often when things are easy, you won't see the need to call upon the Lord for help and strength, but when faced with a more difficult task you will seek Him more fervently. God desires that you seek Him all the time, and He, in His perfect wisdom, will use the more trying circumstances of your life to draw you to Himself.

Will you, with serious consideration and faithful diligence, seek to fulfill the priorities God has for you in His Word? Will you ask Him for help and strength to maintain *the* mindset necessary to put God's priorities into practice in your life? God always helps His children obey His will. He will help you too!

1. In Titus 2:4 we read that older women are to encourage younger women. The word *encourage* is rich with meaning. It carries the idea of training another to be sober-minded about one's duties or responsibilities. What do the Scriptures say about who is to be sober-minded? See 1 Thessalonians 5:8; 1 Timothy 3:2,11; Titus 1:7-8; 2:2,4-6.

2. Why is it so important to be sober-minded? See 1 Thessalonians 5:2,6; Titus 2:11-14; 1 Peter 4:7; and 5:8.

3. According to Titus 2:3-5, in what areas are women to be sensible and serious?

4. What major factor contributes to a prudent and sensible spirit? See Psalms 37:31; 119:9-11; and Proverbs 2:6-7.

5. What does the emphasis on sober-mindedness teach us about our duties listed in Titus 2:3-5?

6. Read Titus 2:3-5 and assess your attitu
living, marriage, parenting, and hom
intent on these areas, training yourself
which areas do you see room for grov

7. What changes or commitments do you need to make so your everyday living will reflect your priorities?

Chapter 3

From Youth to Maturity

"Middle age is when your age starts to show around your middle."

BOB HOPE

"Forty is the old age of youth; fifty the youth of old age."

VICTOR HUGO

"At twenty we worry about what others think of us; at forty we don't care about what others think of us; at sixty we discover they haven't been thinking about us at all."

AUTHOR UNKNOWN

"Old age is like everything else. To make a success of it, you've got to start young."

FRED ASTAIRE

Jokes on aging abound. Some make us smile, while others—depending on our age—hit a bit too close to home so that we inwardly exclaim, *Hey, wait a minute, that's true of me!* Joking around about our age can help take away some of the sting of getting older, and may in some measure prepare us for aging. And one of the struggles women face with aging is losing their youthful beauty.

My dad sought to combat a dependence upon looks by employing a special parenting device we affectionately termed "Dad's Lectures." Lecture #39 was, "It's better to have character than beauty." As a teenage girl I readily agreed with Lecture #39 for a couple reasons. First, while I wasn't a mud fence, I was no great beauty either, so I figured it would be wise to work on the character aspect of my life. And second, I assented to Lecture #39 because I didn't have any wrinkles yet! I thought a few wrinkles would look rather glamorous; however, in my youthful folly I didn't realize that we don't get to choose the *placement* of our wrinkles. Who would have thought that wrinkles would attach themselves to my face in such inconvenient places? What happened to the few distinguished "crow's feet" that would appear only at the outer corners of my eyes and give the appearance of character and wisdom without making me look old?

It is safe to say our modern culture is obsessed with youthfulness. Getting older is tolerated as long as you look younger than your age! As always, the "darling" attitudes of the world run counterclockwise to how God would have us think. The world prizes youth and beauty, and barely acknowledges character and the wisdom and usefulness that come to those who have lived life. However, character and wisdom are far more important to God.

The Ministry of Older Women

If ever there was a place to examine our attitudes about youthfulness and aging it is within God's Word. There is no better place to tackle those issues than within the pages of Scripture. There we see that God places them on the table, out in the open, so we can examine our heart attitudes and see if they line up with the attitudes God would have us possess.

For every woman, the examination process begins now because Titus 2:3-4 states *older* women are to encourage the *younger* women. If we are going to properly do our jobs by encouraging and being encouraged, then we need to respond rightly to each other, whether young or old, and gain insight into how God uses people of all ages to help us grow.

Rather than drawing us together, the differences in our ages often separate us. "Birds of a feather flock together" is an old adage, and it continues to hold true when it comes to spending time with people our own age. Generally we feel more comfortable with those in our same generation. They understand our jokes, our cultural references, and our life circumstances because they share many of the same experiences we have faced.

Even within the body of Christ segregation by age occurs. Many churches have Sunday school classes arranged according to age or station in life. While this pragmatic arrangement has many benefits, it does have a downside as well. We miss out on getting to know those outside our age group. But God has inserted into His Word instruction for overcoming age segregation. It is His design for people of all ages and life situations to minister to one another in the church body. And that is exactly what we find in Titus 2:3-5, where we read that God desires the older women to train the younger women in the art of godly living.

Acknowledging the Age Barriers

God's plan for us includes a teaching and training ministry by the older women to the younger women, but real life often doesn't match up to the ideal. Some older women are reluctant to spend time with younger women. They are hesitant, even a little suspicious of the younger women, almost fearful that the younger women will reject them. The younger women, on the other hand, often feel intimidated by the older women. They feel too young and inexperienced to have anything to say and struggle to find something in common to discuss with those older than themselves.

One of the sweet side effects I have experienced from teaching ladies' Bible studies is watching friendships form between the older and younger women. Gradually the inner lives of both younger and older women are revealed as they share prayer requests and study the Scriptures together. Each week of interaction strengthens the respect and affection between the generations. I love to watch the looks of delight on the young women's faces as they catch a glimpse of the "girl" who resides within an older woman's body. That is the moment when the young women realize they are not so different from the older women after all. It is the moment when the older woman's ministry begins to affect the hearts and lives of the younger women. For example, June is a spry senior citizen who attends our church. She has influenced a number of young women by her life and love for the Lord. Young women consider her their *friend* and look to her as an example. They simply love spending time with her, even though there is a span of 30, 40, even 50 years between them!

What's her secret to effective ministry? It is her passion for Jesus Christ, which has not dimmed through the years. She is genuinely interested in people and eagerly jumps into conversations about Christ. It would be great if we were all like June, but some of us are still fenced in by the age barrier. We need to discover how we can get past that roadblock and begin to engage in effective, multiage ministry.

Ways to Overcome the Age Barriers

No matter what your age, you can develop meaningful relationships with older or younger women who will strengthen and encourage you in your walk with the Lord. Whenever one of us in our family feels reluctant or shy about attending a gathering or reaching out to someone, we encourage that person by saying, "Half of ministry is showing up, and another 25 percent happens when we say hi to someone." Showing up and starting a conversation with someone is where ministry begins and is the baby step to overcoming any age barriers we may face when it comes to ministering to one another in a Titus 2 manner.

You might say, "But I don't know how to converse beyond 'Hi.'" I felt like that for many years myself, but my desire to overcome those disconcerting conversation silences motivated me to do something about it. So I *listened* to those women who seemed gifted in making others feel welcome and at ease. I tried to determine why their conversations moved along so easily while mine felt stilted and awkward. Eventually I discovered a pattern: They asked a question, received a response, then they shared some information about themselves, repeating the process many times during the course of the conversation. I noticed they asked similar kinds of questions at the beginning of a conversation to get the ball rolling—questions like, "So, what have you been doing today?" "Read any good books lately?" "I'm trying to decide what to make for dinner. What are you making?" Now I had some practical conversation starters I could use.

I have a friend who manages to overcome the age barrier by "cruising" the church grounds, foyer, and hallways looking for women who are sitting by themselves, or women who look lost and seem in need of a friend. As she visits with different women and learns their stories, she is able to encourage them in true Titus 2 fashion. God caused the walls of Jericho to fall by the faith of the Israelites, and God can cause age barriers to be swept away as you step out in faith and seek to encourage other women in the Lord.

The Godly Older Woman's Age

People always want to know just how old the "older women" are in Titus 2:3-4 so they'll know which camp they belong to. We can unravel this intriguing little mystery with the help of a bit of logical reasoning based on what's said in verses 4 and 5.

In verse 4 we are told the older women are to train the younger women how to love their husbands and children. This tells us the older woman is someone who has been married long enough to provide insight and practical help to a younger woman about her marriage. And having passed through the stages of parenting, she can also provide counsel about raising children. We can also ascertain from verse 5 that older women have learned how to run their own homes efficiently, and they possess wisdom and experience they can pass on to the younger women.

Other clues as to the older woman's age are found in 1 Timothy 5:1-4,9. There, Paul gave instructions for how Timothy was to appeal to the "older women" as he would his mother. The younger women were to be treated as sisters. This tells us that Timothy, as their "brother," was close in age to the younger women. As a "young man" Timothy could have been in his twenties to forties, so the older women whom he treated as "mothers" would have been twice his age, possibly ranging from their forties on up. We're starting to unravel the mystery about the older woman's age! Let's see what else we can learn.

Paul gave instructions about the care of widows in the church (1 Timothy 5). If possible, each widow's children or grandchildren were to care for her. If, however, she had no family, and was 60 years old or older, and of godly reputation, the church was to step in to care for her needs. We find an additional age clue from Paul when he referred to himself as "aged" when he wrote the book of Philemon while he was in his sixties.

We've done it! We've solved the mystery about the older women as defined in Titus 2:3-5. Without stating a specific age, we can safely say the older women are those who have passed through the seasons of life that the younger women are still passing through. They are old enough to speak to their younger counterparts as someone who has "been there."

Though Paul had in mind older-age women ministering to younger-age women, there is a sense in which *any* woman who has *been there* can speak to other women about the priorities of Titus 2:3-5. What that means for you younger women is that you don't have to wait until you've reached a certain age in life to begin mentoring other women in God's priorities. As you grow in spiritual maturity and life wisdom, you can encourage and train the women coming behind you. The Lord will give you opportunities as you show yourself faithful to implement His priorities in your life. You can pattern your ministry upon the one detailed for the older women in Titus 2:3-5. Let's take a look at the ministry God intends for the older woman, which should be the aim of *every* woman.

The Ministry of the Godly Older Woman

Because of the wisdom older women have gained from their life experiences, they can help the younger women grow in the godly disciplines of Titus 2. God's priorities have been the older woman's priorities, and she has applied herself diligently to them. First Timothy 5:1-10 provides a picture of what this looked like. In that passage the godly older woman was described as fixing her hope on God, praying diligently, and being faithful in her marriage and the raising of her children. She was also known for her acts of service and hospitality, and being devoted to every good work. She learned, over the years, how to practice God's priorities for women.

Even if you didn't become a Christian until recently and your former life was not characterized in any way by striving after God's priorities, you can still begin the process of ministering to the other women

God places in your life. Remember, God saved you to serve others. Though your past may be dark and grim, God ultimately uses all things for good (Romans 8:28). Sometimes the most effective thing you can say to another woman is, "Don't do what I did. I blew it, and faced difficult consequences as a result." No matter how short a time you have known the Lord, you can still encourage women to pursue God's priorities along with you.

The Godly Older Woman's Spiritual Vitality

While the world touts retirement and "pamper me" attitudes for empty nesters, it is God's design for us older believers to share our accumulated biblical wealth and life wisdom with others. In fact, the Bible knows nothing of retirement. In the spiritual realm, some of our most productive years come later in life. The biblical example is one of spiritual vitality and usefulness till both feet slip into the grave.

We read in Job 12:12 that "wisdom is with aged men, with long life is understanding." That tells us we get better with age, and more able to minister to others wisely. In Psalm 92:14 the psalmist praises the Lord while extolling the virtues of the righteous who "still yield fruit in old age," being "full of sap and very green." The righteous will always yield fruit—no matter what their age. They are not withering away, but growing in spiritual vitality, health, flexibility, and wisdom. Believers don't stagnate because God keeps working in them (Philippians 1:6). The normal pattern for every Christian is to bear abundant spiritual fruit in the way a well-trimmed grapevine eventually produces a great harvest of grapes. As we spend time with the Lord and apply His Word to our lives, we will bear fruit—at every age!

The Endurance of the Godly Older Woman

It's encouraging to read about the examples in the Scriptures of godly men and women who followed and served the Lord with passion and zeal into their twilight years. Moses was 80 years old when God called him out of the wilderness to return to Egypt and lead the nation of Israel into the Promised Land. He faithfully led the people of Israel until the day he died. Deuteronomy 34:7 sums up his later years, stating, "Although Moses was one hundred and twenty years old when he died, his eye was not dim, nor his vigor abated." He was still going strong at 120 years. Just think about going on a forty-year camping trip as you enter your eighties!

Many women quit serving or serve very little in their latter years, convincing themselves they have paid their dues or believing their time for ministry is over because they are *too old*. Don't let anything tempt you to retire when you have more to offer than ever! Moses' example is a testimony of the strength God gives us when we step out in faith and trust Him.

Moses' successor, Joshua, was at least middle-aged when he took over for Moses and led the people of Israel into the Promised Land of Canaan. After they entered the land he led the nation on a sustained military campaign before dying at 110 years of age.

Joshua's buddy, Caleb, didn't retire either. He was still vigorous at 85 when the nation entered Canaan. Caleb eagerly fought for his allotment of land in one of the most difficult regions to conquer. You can almost hear the energy in his voice as you read his words in Joshua 14:11: "I am still as strong today as I was in the day Moses sent me; as my strength was then, so my strength is now, for war and for going out and coming in." Caleb knew he was in for a battle against the inhabitants of Canaan, but he believed the Lord would help him conquer the land he had waited so long to receive. He didn't consider his age an impediment, and neither should we.

Other examples of spiritually vibrant older people include Zacharias, Simeon, and Anna, all of whom lived during the time of Jesus' birth. All were known for their devotion to the Lord and their faithful service in prayer.

You may be approaching the age when you can retire from your job if you work outside the home, which you are free to do. But retire from serving the Lord and His people? Never! The men and women we have just surveyed modeled godliness, devotion, zeal, and service until the day of their death. They teach us that passion and fervent devotion to the Lord characterize believers of any age.

Older women, we have no excuse. Many of God's choice and

faithful servants were of the "older" category. God doesn't show partiality toward one age group over another, which is a powerful motivation for us to continue to minister to and serve others. God's people love serving others, and love Him more and more as they grow in maturity and age. So as *we* grow in spiritual maturity and greater love for our Lord, we can minister to other women more than ever. God will strengthen you for the ministry He brings your way.

Developing a Proper Mindset Toward Those Older than Ourselves

Because God uses older, mature believers to teach and train younger women, it's important that the younger women develop a proper mindset toward older women so they can receive their help and counsel. In Leviticus 19:32, God instructs us to show respect and honor to the aged, to those who are "gray-headed." The book of Proverbs twice says that gray hair is a crown of glory and honor (Proverbs 16:31; 20:29).

But how do we show honor to those who are older? One way is to *listen* to them, which shows respect for their years. Proverbs 23:22 states, "Listen to your father who begot you, and do not despise your mother when she is old."

Paul gave similar advice to Timothy. When an older man or woman needed to be rebuked, Timothy was to treat them as he would his father or mother—carefully and respectfully, appealing to them to turn from their sin. He was not to rebuke them sharply. This teaches us the proper attitude to have when ministering to women who are older than ourselves. We should never tolerate sin in their lives, yet we must also show older women respect as we minister to them.

We can show honor to older women by seeking their counsel and developing friendships with them. How we do this depends in part on our individual personalities, giftedness, and resources, but every one of us is called to minister to and show respect to the older women in our lives. When we develop an attitude of respect and honor toward those older than ourselves it primes the pump for us to receive the refreshing waters of wisdom that come from their years of walking with the Lord.

Let's seek ways to show honor and respect to those who are older than ourselves, for this finds favor with God (Leviticus 19:32).

Developing a Proper Mindset Toward Those Younger than Ourselves

As a general rule, we do get wiser with age, but often the young women lead the way in their diligent pursuit of godly wisdom and biblical understanding. In 1 Timothy 4:12 Paul reminded those who were younger that their age didn't have to be a liability. Those who were younger were to be exemplary in "speech, conduct, love, faith and purity." What an encouragement to know a young person can serve as an example to those much older than themselves! The psalmist praised God for this, saying, "I understand more than the aged, because I have observed Your precepts" (Psalm 119:100). In God's kingdom, any person who leans upon God's Word and applies it to their life is an example of wisdom lived out. This is encouraging news no matter what our age!

It can be difficult for an older person to receive encouragement and instruction from a younger person, but it's helpful to remember that God has often used young people in His plans. When the Lord dispatched Samuel to anoint the next king of Israel, Samuel assumed God would choose Eliab, the oldest of Jesse's sons. But God passed over Eliab and his six brothers before revealing His choice in David, the youngest of all Jesse's sons. God knows there is a tendency to dismiss the young as not having anything to say or contribute, yet He has often chosen the youngest, the most unlikely one, to serve as His choice instrument.

> Young or old or in-between, women can encourage other women in the lovely art of following God's priorities.

Some other young people in the Bible who showed great wisdom and godly character were Joseph, Samuel, King Josiah, Daniel and his three friends (Shadrach, Meshach, and Abednego), Jesus' mother Mary, Timothy, and Titus. Within God's kingdom, neither youth *nor* old age discredits a person from being a blessing to others. A person gains favor in God's eyes when he or she humbly leans on the Lord and seeks Him. Age is not a liability!

In Titus 2 Paul exhorted Titus to teach and train *everyone* in the church. Paul didn't single out the younger men and women as being more needy of instruction than the older men and women. If you are in the church, you need instruction regardless of your age. Every believer must be taught. We all must grow in sound doctrine as well as the ability to apply our knowledge to life's circumstances.

God desires women to share the practical day-to-day details of His priorities with one another. Primarily the older women are to take the lead on this because they have wisdom and experience they can impart to the young women. Yet the young women can serve as excellent examples of living out God's priorities. The younger women can also minister to those the Lord brings into their lives. Young or old or in-between, women can encourage other women in the lovely art of following God's priorities.

The Choices of a Lifetime

There's no doubt about it—we are to serve as examples of godly living for one another. And Scripture tells us in many places to live lives that others can imitate, while Titus 2:3-5 provides us with a picture of what that might look like through the example of godly older women. To a certain degree it's easy to tackle the older woman part. All we need to do is wait! The harder part is becoming a *Titus 2* older woman and learning to apply God's Word with skill and humility to life's situations.

In Psalm 90, as Moses contemplated the brevity of life, he asked God on behalf of Israel to "teach us to number our days, that we may present to You a heart of wisdom" (verse 12). Taking stock of our days causes us to live for the Lord and seek *His* wisdom because we become aware of the brevity of life—what is valuable, and what is not. God's wisdom—not our own, nor the world's—is to guide us through life. And then at the end of our days we will *present* to God a heart of wisdom. We can lay the treasure of a lifetime of wisdom and godly living on the altar as a love offering to the Lord.

One Old Testament woman who learned to number her days and was able to offer up to the Lord her heart of wisdom was Ruth. Remember her? She earned a reputation as a woman of excellence because of the choices she made and her godly character. The choices we make today lay the groundwork for the kind of woman we will become. And like Ruth, we can gain the reputation of being women of excellence at any age!

But being a Ruth to those around you means constantly taking stock of your life. A Ruth asks, "What disciplines do I need to put into practice so I can live as an example and blessing to others?" Think about that for a moment. To what degree are you currently displaying the qualities listed in Titus 2:3-5? To what degree do you want those qualities to distinguish you in the future? Once you have identified the areas you need to work on, then ask, "What steps must I take to get me to where God wants me to be?"

Dwight L. Moody said, "Preparation for old age should begin not later than one's teens. A life which is empty of purpose until 65 will not suddenly become filled on retirement."[1] What wise counsel! If we take Moody's advice, we must consider the steps that will lead us to our goal. For example, an older woman is to be a model of reverent behavior, which is all well and good, but how do we get to that place? Let's start at the very beginning.

First, Seek Salvation

The first step to spiritual growth is salvation. Without true, life-changing salvation, the fundamental building blocks for a godly life are missing. We cannot manufacture godly fruit apart from God's saving grace. The Bible says at salvation, we are made into "a new creature" in Christ (2 Corinthians 5:17). Before salvation, we are spiritually dead (Ephesians 2:1-3). Just as a dead tree never grows, neither does a spiritually dead person.

Ponder these questions to get started: How do you know you are saved? What are you trusting in to get you into heaven? Has Jesus Christ changed you into a new creature? Are you born again?

If you don't know how to answer those questions, then today is the day to seek the Lord while He may be found (Isaiah 55:6). God sent His Son, Jesus, into the world to save you from the consequences of your sin, making it possible for you to live with Him in heaven. Romans 5:8 says, "God demonstrates His own love toward us, in that while we were yet sinners, Christ died for us." All we must do to receive this magnificent gift is believe in Him. And if we do, we "shall not perish, but have eternal life" (John 3:16). For salvation is "by grace... through faith" (Ephesians 2:8). We must turn to God in faith, repent of our sins, and place our faith in Christ to take away that sin. Romans 10:9 states, "If you confess with your mouth Jesus as Lord, and believe in your heart that God raised Him from the dead, you will be saved." He will save you and help you to follow Him, if you ask Him.

Second, Seek God's Word

If you have placed your faith in the Lord Jesus Christ alone for salvation, believing He died for you and rose from the dead, you have taken the first step! A growing love for and dependence upon God's Word is the next step to spiritual growth. God uses His Word to teach you about Himself and His ways. There's just no substitute for getting to know the Lord through His Word. It is *the* primary source for spiritual growth.

At a minimum you need to read the Bible each day and have a quiet time or a devotion time with God. A quiet time is when you spend time with the Lord hearing what He has to say through His Word, and then you talk with Him through prayer. Because the Word of God is the principal means God uses to transform you into His image, the more you dig into His Word and let it "richly dwell within you" (Colossians 3:16), the more you will grow and fall in love with its Author.

Third, Seek to Be Rid of Sin

The third step to spiritual maturity is a willingness to lay aside sin and anything that distracts or entangles you. Though you are called to turn away from sin at salvation, it is also a lifelong discipline you have to practice. A woman who spends time in the Word each day is going to see her sin like she sees her reflection in a mirror. The closer she gets to the mirror of God's Word, the more she will see the sin in her life that needs to be dealt with. The Word of God is living, active, and sharper than a two-edged sword, and it gets into the core of your being, judging even the thoughts and intentions of your heart (Hebrews 4:12). As you submit yourself to the Word of God, you are transformed more and more into the likeness of Christ.

Fourth, Seek to Obey God

The fourth step toward growing in godliness comes when you obey God. At its most basic level, obedience is simply discovering the ways the Lord wants you to follow Him through His Word and then doing those things out of love for Him. Your obedience to God is what sets you apart and marks you as a Christian, as the apostle John says in 1 John 2:3: "By this we know that we have come to know Him, if we keep His commandments." For example, God's Word says we aren't to lie (Colossians 3:9), so in *obedience* we put off lying and seek to speak truthfully.

Believers obey God. It isn't always easy to obey the Lord and we don't do it perfectly, but the Lord does help us to obey Him. The Lord has given every believer a "survival kit" for obedience. Our survival kit consists of the Holy Spirit, who is given to every believer at salvation. He helps and strengthens us to do God's will. The Bible is also part of our survival kit. Without God's Word we wouldn't know how to obey the Lord. God has also provided the preaching and teaching of His Word and the fellowship of other believers to encourage us to do what's right. Each one of the items in our survival kit helps us to obey the Lord.

But even then we must seek the Lord's assistance and obey His Word while relying on His grace. Paul, in 1 Corinthians 15:10, said, "By the grace of God I am what I am, and His grace toward me did not prove vain; but I labored even more than all of them, yet not I, but the grace of God with me." Paul mastered the art of diligently serving the Lord, all the while leaning on Him for strength and grace to live for His glory.

Salvation, studying God's Word, confessing sin, and seeking to obey the Lord are the building blocks to growing in godliness. No believer

ever gets past the stage of needing to take in the Scriptures. No believer ever gets to the place where she does not battle her sin. Every believer needs to continue to obey the Lord—at any age and at every stage of the Christian life. These are the basics to growing in godliness and becoming a lovely picture of the Titus 2 woman.

Seek Out Relationships with Other Women

And with those steps to spiritual growth in place we are ready to build into each other's lives in true Titus 2:3-5 fashion! Older women, who do you have a Titus 2 relationship with? Your daughter or daughter-in-law? Maybe a friend in a Bible study? Perhaps someone you've met at church? God's plan is to use godly older women to build up the younger women in Christ. Do you have younger women in your life?

Younger women, are you getting to know the older women in your church? Are you seeking to learn from their wisdom and experience? Think of the life questions you can ask an older woman the next time you find yourself sitting together. Begin to glean the wisdom she has accumulated through the years so you can benefit from it in your own life.

Don't let age get in the way of the ministry God intends for you to have with the women around you. It's God's plan for the older women to teach and train the younger women in the priorities of Titus 2:3-5. Keep seeking the Lord, spending time with Him in His Word, and obeying Him, and you will become the kind of woman other women will seek out because *you* are a Titus 2 woman!

1. What do you learn from the following verses about age and spiritual vitality? Job 12:12; Psalms 71:6-9,17-18; 92:14; and 148:12-13.

2. Look up the following verses to see how the aged served God's people. Note their age, if possible, and how they served others: Deuteronomy 34:5-7; Joshua 14:6-12; 24:29; Luke 1:5-9; and 2:36-38.

3. God doesn't put older believers on the shelf and we shouldn't either! If you are an older woman, how did the verses from the two questions above encourage or challenge you to press on in serving others?

4. If you are younger, how did the verses from the two questions above encourage you? How did they challenge your thinking about the spiritual vitality of the aged?

5. What are two or three ways you can convey an attitude of honor and respect toward the aged?

6. If you are a young woman, ask yourself, "Am I living in such a way now that I will be qualified to teach the younger women someday?" And, "What priorities do I need to work on more so that I will possess the godly qualities of Titus 2 when I am older?"

7. If you are an older woman, ask yourself, "Am I living according to the priorities of Titus 2:3-5? Do I possess the qualities listed in Titus 2:3-5?" If not, consider what steps you can take so you can begin to live this way.

8. The goal for every woman, whatever her age, is to live according to God's priorities. And we have the privilege of following those priorities *all* of our lives! What disciplines and habits do you have now that will aid your spiritual growth in the long term?

Part 2

The Art of Following God's Priorities

Chapter 4

The Art of Growing in Holiness

E sther trembled as she stood in the doorway of the king's inner court. Though she wore her royal robes, they did not bolster her courage, for it had been over a month since she had been summoned by the king. She knew well the consequences of appearing in his presence without being summoned: Anyone who dared to enter without being called for was put to death unless the king extended his scepter to that person. Yet necessity—no, survival—demanded that she dare break court protocol and go to the king to beg his help. Her life, and the lives of her people, hung in the balance of the king's willingness to extend mercy. So it calmed her somewhat to remember how she and all the Jews of Susa had not eaten any food nor had anything to drink for the last three days as they prayed to God to grant her mission success.

Esther had prepared herself spiritually, mentally, and physically to go to the king. She was as ready as she would ever be. Now it was her desire that her every move, her every word would show her respect for the king's power and position as she stood waiting. One of the king's advisors whispered something in his ear. Her breath caught. *So now he knew*. He knew she was standing there in his court *without* an invitation from him. The presumption of it appalled her, but she knew there was no other way. As her cousin Mordecai had reminded her, "Who knows whether you have not attained royalty for such a time as this?" (Esther 4:14). For a barest moment the king's eyes met Esther's, then she hurriedly cast her eyes downward to show her respect. "Queen Esther, come forward," he announced as he extended his scepter toward her.[1]

Esther well understood the value of respectful behavior. For it communicates to others that someone or something is of great importance. And though we may never find ourselves in a situation like Esther's, we must learn all we can about reverent behavior, for it is one of the first priorities listed in Titus 2:3-5. We're going to take a look at what reverent behavior is, why it is necessary for women today, and what it will look like when it's implemented in our lives on a daily basis. That will enable us to show, just like Esther, that we understand the value of respectful behavior.

What Reverent Behavior Means

Paul began Titus 2:3 with this instruction: "Older women likewise are to be reverent in their behavior." "Likewise" can also be translated "similarly" or "in like manner," which means Paul's instructions for the older women are *connected* to his instructions to the older men. One verse earlier he had exhorted the men to "be temperate, dignified, sensible, sound in faith, in love, in perseverance," and then he urged the women—*in the same way or in a similar manner*—to be reverent in their behavior. The older men were to serve as models of godly and mature character, which is exactly what Paul desired for the older women.

Now, though Paul addressed his comments to the older women, these priorities, including the call to reverence, are for *all* women. "Why?" you might ask. Because young women end up becoming older women without even trying. So it's reasonable to suppose if there are specific commands given to the older women, then the younger women need to know what they are, begin taking them into consideration, and work at applying them to their lives so those qualities will be true of them when they finally become older. In other words, *this command is for all women.*

The King James Version of the Bible translates the command in Titus 2:3 this way: "The aged women likewise, that they be in behaviour as becometh holiness." The mention of behavior adds a nuance of meaning to our understanding of this command. We could summarize it this way: Women are to act in a way that *fits in* with holiness.

The New International Version translates this verse in a similar manner: "Teach the older women to be reverent in the way they live." The Amplified Bible provides well-rounded insight into this instruction by stating, "Bid the older women similarly to be reverent and devout in their deportment as becomes those engaged in sacred service." By examining different Bible translations we learn that reverence is seen by the *way we live*.

Even if we learn nothing else about reverent behavior, we have ascertained this much: Our lives must match what we profess about Christ. We are to *walk the talk* and practice what we preach. I am reminded of this whenever I go to the doctor's office and see the "health professionals" standing outside the building puffing away on their cigarettes. The incongruity between their profession and their actions always strikes me.

We must not allow for disparity between our profession of faith in Jesus Christ and our actions. This concept countermands the idea that all that matters with God is our heart. Many who say, "I am saved. I am forgiven. God knows my heart" usually do so because their actions aren't what they ought to be. Sadly, comments like that reveal a person's misunderstanding of the fact a saved life results in a changed life. God does indeed see our hearts, but that does not excuse our disobedient behavior. Being saved, obeying the Lord, and showing a changed life are all the same thing. Salvation can, should, and does have an effect upon a believer's everyday life. Jesus said in John 10:27, "My sheep hear My voice, and I know them, and they follow Me." Jesus expects us to follow Him, not merely profess to do so! We imitate Him by living a reverent life.

What Reverent Behavior Looks Like

"To be reverent in their behavior" encompasses the idea of sacred and holy duties performed in everyday living. It does not point to a specific behavior, but includes all aspects of our demeanor. Because it's not specific to any one aspect of behavior it's a difficult concept to pin down and apply, but that doesn't mean we can't come to understand this phrase or how to practice it. Let's begin first by understanding what reverent behavior is.

To show reverence toward someone or something means to have a deep respect or awe. When we respect something we protect it, we care for it, we treat it differently than those items that don't garner our reverence. Women are called to reverent *behavior,* which means showing reverence in our actions. The dictionary defines *behavior* as "a manner of conducting oneself."[2] I like to think of behavior as the outward expression of our inner attitudes.

Proverbs 31:30 helps define reverent behavior when it sums up the life of the godly woman: "Charm is deceitful and beauty is vain, but a woman who fears the Lord, she shall be praised." A woman who fears or reverences the Lord will act accordingly in her daily life. She is careful with her speech and considers her actions because her love for God hems in her behavior.

> God's plan has always been for every one of His children to look like they belong to Him.

First Timothy 2:9-10 helps explain why. God says, "I want women to adorn themselves with proper clothing, modestly and discreetly, not with braided hair and gold or pearls or costly garments, but rather by means of good works, as is proper for women making a claim to godliness." What does that mean for you and me? It means when we make a claim to godliness—when we call ourselves Christians and followers of Jesus Christ—then our lives should line up with our proclamation. We wouldn't want someone to exclaim, "Really? You are a Christian? I never would have guessed that!" Our reverent *behavior* authenticates our *words*—that we are followers of Jesus.

God's plan has always been for every one of His children to look like they belong to Him. How can people tell we are His children? *By what we say and do.* As believers we are new creatures in Christ—the old things have passed away and new things have come. A whole new way of living is available to us through Jesus Christ, which is exactly what Paul said when he quoted some Old Testament texts in 2 Corinthians 6:16-17: "God said, 'I will dwell in them and walk among them; and I will be their God, and they shall be My people. Therefore, come out from their midst and be separate,' says the Lord." When God is our Father, He calls us to a new life and a new way of living.

The Reason for Reverence

Curiosity makes us want to know the *who* and the *why* before we *do*. Often, being able to associate a face with a name makes all the difference for us when it comes to praying for someone, or when we learn more about their story it helps us serve them more willingly and wholeheartedly. And for some of us, just knowing *who* we need to show reverence *toward* makes all the difference in our attitude about reverent behavior.

Thankfully, the Lord provides that information! Our reverent behavior has a focus, and it is hinted at in Titus 2:5 when Paul supplies the proper motivation for everything we do: "that the Word of God will not be dishonored." What a mighty and humbling thought! Our lives can either honor or dishonor God's Word. We bring honor to His Word when we live according to it, and we dishonor His Word when we rebel against it.

The motivation of bringing honor to the Lord, which Paul whispered in verse 5, was shouted from the rooftops in verses 11-14:

> The grace of God has appeared, bringing salvation to all men,
> instructing us to deny ungodliness and worldly desires and
> to live sensibly, righteously and godly in the present age,
> looking for the blessed hope and the appearing of the glory
> of our great God and Savior, Christ Jesus, who gave Himself
> for us to redeem us from every lawless deed, and to purify
> for Himself a people for His own possession, zealous for
> good deeds.

We show reverence to God out of grateful love and devotion to Him for all He has done for us! He freely gave us salvation by grace through faith in His Son, Jesus Christ, who sacrificed His life for us. He didn't have to do this, and we certainly didn't deserve it. Our salvation allows us to be God's own people, and as His people we are to reflect His nature.

Understanding the debt of love and gratitude we owe to our kind heavenly Father helps motivate us to obey and love Him more readily and faithfully. The fact He has done so much for us makes us want to do whatever He asks. We will still have times when we find it difficult to obey the Lord, but the desire to show our love and gratitude to Him will override our tendency to rebel.

Charles Spurgeon had wise words to say about how gratitude moves us to action. Commenting on how our service becomes an offering and an opportunity to give to our heavenly Father, he said:

> To wash feet may be servile, but to wash His feet is royal work. To unloose the shoe-latchet is poor employ, but to unloose the great Master's shoe is a princely privilege. The shop, the barn, the scullery, and the smithy become temples when men and women do all to the glory of God! Then "divine service" is not a thing of a few hours and a few places, but all life becomes holiness unto the Lord, and every place and thing, as consecrated as the tabernacle and its golden candlestick.[3]

Spurgeon hit the nail on the head with regard to showing reverent behavior. When everything we do is done because of the love God showed us, then our every action, conversation, and thought is transformed to become an act of worship and love for our King.

Reverent Behavior Begins with a Reverent Mind

Because we are to live in a way that brings glory to God, we need to understand exactly how to implement reverent behavior in our lives. The first step for any spiritual pursuit begins in our minds and hearts. *What we think about something determines how we respond or act.* Proverbs 23:7, which speaks of the selfish man, states this principle: "As he thinks within himself, so he is." Solomon was saying that what we think and ponder upon reveals our true nature and, ultimately, affects our behavior.

So it is essential that we think on the right things, which is why growing in reverent behavior is a lot like making soup. When we make soup, we start with a few fresh ingredients and let them simmer and interact with each other. Later we add more flavors and items that further enhance the flavor of the soup—until it is ready to serve to our family and friends.

If we were to make a big pot of "Reverent Behavior Soup" we would need to choose the best ingredients to ensure our thoughts produced the most "flavorful" behavior. All reverent behavior begins with a hefty dose of *love for God*, a love so fresh and strong that it permeates your heart and soul (Deuteronomy 6:5). We should follow that with a liberal helping of the *Word of God* because it is Scripture that produces reverence for God (Psalm 119:38). Then we would need to add a good amount of *seek first His kingdom and His righteousness* (Matthew 6:33), and a generous helping of *setting your mind on the things above* (Colossians 3:1-3). We could also add liberal handfuls of *whatever is true, honorable, right, pure, lovely, of good repute, excellent, and worthy of praise* (Philippians 4:8). These ingredients make the soup robust and heartwarming. We'll need to give special attention to the *renewing of our mind* (Romans 12:2). This ingredient is essential to the stew and causes every other flavor to stand out. And then, as with all good soups and stews, those ingredients must simmer in our minds so that over time they produce a veritable feast of reverent behavior.

What we think on leads to how we act. This is such a simple truth, but one that is overlooked far too often. It is much easier to deal with the more concrete areas of our behavior than it is to address our more ephemeral thoughts. Yet if we hope to live reverently as God desires that we do, then we must take a look at how we think and train ourselves in the art of cultivating a reverent mind.

Ways to Train Your Mind

While our Reverent Behavior Soup is the stuff of fiction, its ingredients are not, and a devoted focus to those qualities will produce a hearty enough meal to satisfy even the most ravenous of eaters. All the ingredients for Reverent Behavior Soup are found in Bible. There is no need to shop anywhere else!

When we spend time in God's Word day after day,
we become perfumed with Christ's likeness.

Our daughter works at a local Starbucks, and when she finishes her shift and walks into the house we smell coffee! Her hair, her clothes, even her car is perfumed with "café parfum." She doesn't roll around in the coffee beans or pour coffee grounds into her apron pockets; she simply shows up for work and goes about her business. *The perfuming happens to her by association.*

The same is true about interacting with God's Word. When we spend time in it day after day, we become perfumed with Christ's likeness. The sweet fragrance of Christ wafts about us even when we are not aware of it. The thoughts that lead to reverent behavior come from mentally marinating ourselves in the things of God, and that marinating occurs when we set aside time to read, study, meditate on, or memorize portions of Scripture and prayerfully seek to apply what we learn to our lives.

How do you make time for the Lord each day? Do you read God's Word on a consistent basis? Do you spend time in prayer and examine your life for any areas of sin that may hinder your walk with Him? Do you attend church regularly? Are you involved in a Sunday school class, Bible study, or small group? Do you listen to sermons on God's Word? If you want to smell like coffee, you need to spend time in the coffee shop. And if you want to live a life pleasing to God, you need to spend time in the place where God explains how to please Him—the Bible.

It seems so simple, doesn't it? Just spend time each day getting God's Word into your mind and heart. But anyone who has desired to have consistent quiet times with God will tell you that making it happen can be a battle. Each day comes with its own set of temptations to do something other than read the Bible. Every morning presents us with the same challenge Joshua gave to the Israelites as they prepared to enter the Promised Land: "Choose for yourselves today whom you will serve" (Joshua 24:15). In effect you are proclaiming, "I choose to serve the Lord" by your simple act of finding a quiet place to read your Bible and pray to the Lord. Your growth in reverence is directly proportional to your intake of the Word of God. Get saturated!

The Beauty of Reverent Behavior

I have known Bridget for nine years, and during that time I have seen a woman transformed. Bridget doesn't sit around watching television and eating bonbons; she is one busy woman! Yet she has still found ways to dwell on God's Word all day long, and that dependence upon the Lord has produced a radical change in her life. The jump in her spiritual life came when she began to memorize and listen to God's Word on an ongoing basis each day. Her spiritual insights are meaty and rich, and her attitudes and behaviors are ever more Christlike. She is literally being transformed from glory to glory into the image of Christ by daily soaking in the Word.

When the Word of God permeates our hearts and minds, our behavior will naturally become reverent. The more our minds are filled with God, the more our behavior will reflect Him. We see from Proverbs 31:30 that a woman characterized by reverent behavior fears the Lord. She understands that a life built upon charm and beauty will soon pass away. It's for that reason that she doesn't obsess over her appearance or use her body to attract attention to herself.

A woman of reverent behavior is characterized by modesty and humility in her dress and demeanor (1 Timothy 2:9-10). From 1 Peter 3:1-6 we learn she patterns her submission after Christ's and values a gentle and quiet spirit, which is precious to God. She is not oblivious or uncaring of her looks, but at the same time, her outward adornment is not her primary focus. Like the Proverbs 31 woman, her focus is on the Lord and how she may please Him.

Even within Titus chapter 2 we gets hints about what a reverent woman's life looks like. We learn she is careful with her words, has self-control, and knows what things are good and pleasing to the Lord and does them. She excels at loving her husband and children and making her home a priority, and helps other women to do the same. She is characterized by prudence and discretion, purity and kindness.

Titus 2:3-5 is just one example of what the daily life of a reverent woman looks like. She is busy, productive, and focused on others. At her core she engages in those delightful duties because she loves and desires to please God. To an observer her life looks directed, focused, and confident simply because she has made it her mission in life to know what God's priorities are for her and to put those priorities into practice each day.

Reverent behavior comes from good doctrine found within the pages of Scripture. Our doctrine determines our behavior. When our doctrine is sound and healthy then our behavior will reflect it. But if we have little doctrine or poorly formed doctrine, then our lives will reflect that as well. We will find it difficult or impossible to live reverently. This is why it is essential that every woman understands the priorities God has for her—that's where growing in reverent behavior begins. The world may change its priorities, but God does not change His. Because God is trustworthy and unchanging, we can embrace His priorities without fear.

> As you present every part of your life to the Lord, it is transformed from the mundane to an act of worship.

How You Can Build a Reverent Life

Even after studying what reverent behavior means and meditating on it, you may find it difficult to pin down any certain action or behavior in your life as being particularly *reverent*. Romans 12:1 is a great help here. It states, "I urge you, brethren, by the mercies of God, to present your bodies a living and holy sacrifice, acceptable to God, which is your spiritual service of worship." As you present every part of your life to the Lord, it is transformed from the mundane to an act of worship. A woman who reverences the Lord understands this.

What will reverent behavior look like in *your* life? I couldn't begin to say what it may look like, but I do know this: It will not run contrary to God's Word. Reverent behavior avoids sin. It falls in line with everything the Scriptures teach.

What Your Reverent Behavior Says About You

When every act of your life is an act of worship to the Lord, then your life simply *becomes* reverent. You don't have to repeat to yourself, "I need to act reverent today. I've got to act reverent today. Help! Why can't I be reverent today?" Reverent behavior flows out of your relationship with the Lord. Reverent behavior is the life response of a woman who knows her soul has been bought with the precious blood of Jesus Christ. She knows she was bought at a price, and that she is not her own (1 Corinthians 6:19-20).

In Titus chapter 3, Paul encouraged Titus to remind the people to live as godly examples by being gentle and considerate to others no matter who they were. Lest we get puffed up and averse to ministering to unbelievers, Paul reminded them—and us—of our past: "We also once were foolish ourselves, disobedient, deceived, enslaved to various lusts and pleasures, spending our life in malice and envy, hateful, hating one another" (verse 3). It's always good to take a look at where we came from! Doing so brings perspective and awakens gratitude, love, and sympathy for the lost. Then Paul went on to remind the believers of God's work in them in verses 4-7:

> When the kindness of God our Savior and His love for mankind appeared, He saved us, not on the basis of deeds which we have done in righteousness, but according to His mercy, by the washing of regeneration and renewing by the Holy Spirit, whom He poured out upon us richly through Jesus Christ our Savior, so that being justified by His grace we would be made heirs according to the hope of eternal life.

Not only does God save those who repent of their sin and place their faith in Christ, He piles blessing upon blessing on them through Jesus Christ. Reverent behavior is the result. Believers respond to God's love, kindness, grace, mercy, and blessing in the only way they can—by living their lives for Him. Charles Spurgeon summed it up this way:

> Be ye holy, for ye serve a holy God. If you were making a present to a prince, you would not find him a lame horse to ride upon; you would not offer him a book out of which leaves had been torn, nor carry him a timepiece whose wheels were broken. No, the best of the best you would give to one whom you honored and loved. Give your very best to your Lord. Seek to be at your best whenever you serve Him.[4]

How you live reveals how you value the life of grace and mercy given to you by God. Your reverent behavior indicates you love the Lord and desire every area of your life to be filled to the brim with Him. It's no wonder God made reverent behavior the first priority in Titus 2:3-5. Reverent behavior declares our love for Him!

Now *that's* a priority we want to put into practice.

1. What is the basis and motivation for reverent behavior?
   See 2 Corinthians 5:14-15; Colossians 3:1-3; and Hebrews
   12:28-29.

2. Proverbs 23:7, in speaking of the selfish man, states this
   principle: "As he thinks within himself, so he is." That is, how
   we think about things influences our behavior. What do the
   following verses say about our thoughts and how we are
   to think? Read Deuteronomy 6:5; Psalm 119:38; Matthew
   6:33; Luke 6:44-45; Romans 12:2; and Philippians 4:8.

3. What is the demeanor of a godly woman? See Proverbs
   31:30; 1 Timothy 2:9-15; and 1 Peter 3:1-6.

4. What attitudes are necessary for reverent behavior?

5. What verses from the questions above have encouraged you toward reverent behavior?

6. What does reverent behavior look like in your life? Try to put into words the behaviors that define reverence in your everyday living.

Chapter 5

The Art of Speaking Pleasant Words

I am not a big fan of science fiction movies, but the boys in our family enjoy that genre, so I have seen my fair share of this kind of movie. During many of these movies there inevitably comes a time when someone gets trapped outside the spacecraft, generally due to a crew member's incompetence or nefarious purposes. For one reason or another, the hero's luckless companion cannot get back inside. The hero races to the spacecraft's hatch door, chest heaving, only to find he is too late—the hatch door is in emergency lockdown mode. He cannot save his friend. He stands at the hatch door window peering helplessly at his buddy trapped outside. Suddenly the spacecraft lurches and the poor fellow outside the spacecraft is knocked from his precarious perch and is set adrift into the black darkness of space. The hero pounds on the window, his hot breath fogging up the glass as he watches his friend float away. He slowly slides down the interior wall in despair and disbelief. There is nothing he can do now to rescue his friend. It is too late.

This scene is horrifying to watch, and even as I write about it I find my mind trying to wriggle away from the fate of that poor astronaut floating away in space. Fortunately, most of us will never face a situation like the one I have described. *However, many of us have, and will, face situations similar to it.*

What situation could we possibly find ourselves in that would be similar to the story above? Here's a clue: It has something to do with *speech.* The next of God's priorities we are going to examine has to do with gossip. But don't worry; all you need to do is take notes. This chapter is perfect for those gals who live back east—or out west, or up north, or down south! After all gossip is what *other* women do. It certainly couldn't be a problem for you and me, *could it*?

No doubt you are aware of gossip. You've heard gossip, you may have been hurt by its effects, and it's possible you may have even gossiped about others. Well, in Titus 2:3 we see that God's next priority for women touches on this very matter: Women are not to be "malicious gossips." Malicious—that sounds so bad! No wonder God desires for women to eradicate this fleshly deed.

Because gossip inevitably will affect us one way or another, and because it's so easy for a conversation to slip into gossip without intending for it to do so, we would benefit from learning more about what God thinks of gossip, its effects, and how we can serve as godly examples in our speech.

Do you remember that when Jesus was instructing the crowds in the Sermon on the Mount, He said something so jaw-dropping people didn't know how to respond? He taught in Matthew 5:21-26 that even if we are merely *angry* at someone we are guilty as though we have committed murder. And merely looking upon a woman with lust makes one *already* guilty of adultery (5:27-28). Jesus wanted the people to realize that everyone was guilty of the sins of adultery and murder because at least once in their lives they had lusted in their hearts or had become angry. The command to not engage in malicious gossip functions in a similar way. Malicious gossip is a big, bad, full-blown sin that begins in seed form in the heart.

With the help of God's Word, we are going to learn what gossip is, its effects, how we can respond when we are the victim of gossip, how we can respond to those who do the gossiping, and finally, how to speak with the graciousness of a Titus 2 woman who seeks to maintain God's priorities in her life.

What Is Malicious Gossip?

When I think of gossip, the picture that often comes to my mind is that of the harmless prattle and lively conjecture of idle women who sally forth from one house to another, meddling in each other's affairs in many a Jane Austen tale. Though their comings and goings often cause trouble, in the end the damage is of no great consequence, and all ends well. Yet that idyllic and even humorous picture of gossip is a far cry from the truth and fails to accurately portray the damage caused by gossip.

The Bible addresses and condemns the whisperings of a talebearer and the idle lifestyle that goes with it (1 Timothy 5:13). Idle talebearing and constant conversation about others is a characteristic of many unbelievers. Yet as believers, we are to put off this kind of conversation, and instead, engage in wholesome, encouraging words that build others up rather than tear them down.

That type of gossip is bad enough, and there is another word that describes a far more serious type of gossip. In Titus 2:3 we are commanded to not be *malicious* gossips. In English we use two words to describe the one Greek word used in Titus 2:3. We are to not be *diabolos*—malicious gossips.[1] You might be wondering right now, *Isn't* diabolos *another name for the devil?* Yes. It literally means to be "devil-speakers," "false accusers," or "slanderers."

A slanderer utters false or malicious lies about someone in order to damage that person's reputation, make herself look good, or gain some kind of advantage. Malicious gossip is vindictive and looks for opportunities to target its victim. Slanderous speech often stems from a bitter, unforgiving heart. No wonder Titus 2:3 tells us not to be malicious gossips!

Revelation 12:10 identifies Satan as the *accuser* of the brethren, while 1 Peter 5:8 identifies him as our *adversary*. When we engage in malicious gossip we are acting like "devils" accusing and slandering others. A scary thought, isn't it? When we act in this manner we earn the reproach of Christ, who said in John 8:44, "You are of your father the devil, and you want to do the desires of your father. He was a murderer from the beginning, and does not stand in the truth because there is no truth in him. Whenever he speaks a lie, he speaks from his own nature, for he is a liar and the father of lies." Our spiritual family lineage can be determined by our speech!

Believers should never engage in malicious gossip or slander. This is what John meant when he said in 1 John 3:10, "By this the children of God and the children of the devil are obvious: anyone who does not practice righteousness is not of God, nor the one who does not love his brother." If we make it a habit to speak like the devil, reveals who our true father is. Therefore, Paul commands believers not to act like the children of the devil, and instead to "put on the new self, which in the likeness of God has been created in righteousness and holiness of the truth" (Ephesians 4:24).

I Would Never Slander Someone!

You might be thinking to yourself, *Engage in malicious gossip? Me? I would never do something like that!* And I hope that is true, but let's face it—even Christians are capable of engaging in slander. Have you ever made an unkind or critical statement about a brother or sister in Christ? Have you ever repeated something about someone else that was false, or at least not completely true? Have you ever slanted statements about someone else to make that person look bad? If you have, then you have engaged in slander. Granted, it's a *mild* form of malicious gossip, but it is still gossip nonetheless.

Did you know it's possible to engage in slander *without uttering a single word* aloud? It's easy to do this; all we need to do is slander others *in our thoughts*. At one point in my walk with the Lord, I became convicted that I was guilty of slanderous thoughts after I read 2 Timothy 2:23, which states, "Refuse foolish and ignorant speculations, knowing that they produce quarrels." I realized that sometimes the conversations I played out in my mind fit into this category. They were nothing more than foolish or ignorant speculations. Maybe you've had "conversations" similar to ones I've had, in which I've engaged in foolish speculations by imagining offenses against me or expecting a wrong response.

Those critical thoughts produce in us a quarrelsome spirit, and that is not at all how God desires believers to act. Second Timothy 2:24 explains how Christians should act—and think: "The Lord's bondservant must not be quarrelsome, but be kind to all, able to teach, patient when wronged." Rather than creating quarrels in our minds, we are to think kind, patient thoughts toward others, *even when we are wronged.*

Then as if that wasn't enough, I read James 5:9, which sealed the deal for me: "Do not complain, brethren, against one another, so that you yourselves may not be judged; behold, the Judge is standing right at the door." I realized that even if I wasn't complaining outwardly about someone, I was still complaining, speculating about, and criticizing them *in my heart.* James emphasizes how serious this sin is by adding that God, the Judge, is standing at the door. Even believers face the sanctifying discipline of the Lord, though we are spared sin's *eternal* consequences because of Christ's righteousness applied to us.

The words we utter on our lips begin in our hearts, which is why we must make even the *content* of our thoughts a priority. If we don't seek to overcome critical, slanderous thoughts, they will almost certainly give birth to malicious gossip. If you find you have been slandering someone in your heart, confess your sin to the Lord, and if necessary, go to the person you have wronged and ask for their forgiveness as well. But whether we speak unkindly, or purposely slander another, we need to face up to the fact that God wants us to speak graciously at all times.

Slander is a serious matter to God. We can see how serious He is about it in the book of Proverbs, which provides insight into God's mind by using some rather strong terms to describe those who engage in slander and gossip. Listen to this: A woman who spreads slander is a *fool*, according to Proverbs 10:18. Being called a fool might not seem so bad, but being labeled a "godless" person who "destroys," "worthless," and an "evildoer" might be enough to make us take a closer look at this command not to gossip (Proverbs 11:9; 16:27; 17:4).

The Effects of Gossip and Slander

David eloquently described the effects of slander in his life in Psalm 31:13: "I have heard the slander of many, terror is on every side; while they took counsel together against me, they schemed to take away my life." David grieved when he heard the slander against him. He was heartbroken by the slander of his "friends," and felt as though his soul and body were wasting away (Psalm 31:9). Maybe you have experienced what David did and know firsthand the devastation and heartbreak that can come from gossip.

The quickest way to undermine unity, harmony, and fellowship among believers is to engage in the lies and deceitful whisperings of gossip. Instead, we are urged to diligently preserve the unity of the Holy Spirit by walking in a manner worthy of our calling, with humility, gentleness, and patience (Ephesians 4:1-3).

Not only was David slandered during his lifetime, but Jesus was falsely accused all throughout His earthly ministry. The apostles were buffeted by this particular trial as well. Peter reminds us that anyone desiring to live a godly life in an ungodly culture will experience the pain of slander and gossip (1 Peter 2:12; 3:16).

How You Should Respond to Slander

So how are we to respond to gossip and slander that may swirl about us at different times in our lives? First, we can console ourselves that we are in good company. Jesus said we are blessed if people insult us and say false things against us. Just like the prophets of old, when we are persecuted in this way, we can rejoice for the reward that awaits us in heaven (Matthew 5:11-12).

Second, when Paul was falsely accused, he commended himself to God as God's servant (2 Corinthians 6:4-8), knowing nothing happened to him without God's approval. We too can entrust ourselves to our all-wise and loving God and respond the same way.

Third, we can follow Paul's example in 1 Corinthians 4:13. When he was slandered, he tried to conciliate with the offended party. The best way to dispel disagreements and misunderstandings is to simply go to the person and try to gain their friendship or goodwill. We can clear up offenses and grievances if we are willing to seek unity with one another.

Fourth, we need to make sure we respond in a godly manner. Peter admonished in 1 Peter 2:12, "Keep your behavior excellent among the Gentiles, so that in the thing in which they slander you as evildoers, they may because of your good deeds, as they observe them, glorify God in the day of visitation." When we are insulted and reviled we are to give a blessing, which will bring shame upon those who slander and falsely accuse us (1 Peter 2:21-23; 3:9,16).

Reminding ourselves that other believers have experienced similar trials, entrusting ourselves to God, seeking to clear up misunderstandings, and responding in a godly way are relatively *passive* ways to respond to slander. There are also some *active* ways we can respond to false and hurtful gossip.

Psalm 34:13 tells us to keep our tongue from evil and our lips from speaking deceit. Make sure *your* speech doesn't turn ugly if you find yourself on the receiving end of malicious gossip.

If you associate with people who are prone to gossip you increase your chances that others will gossip about you. So limit the time you spend with such people. You will also need to use discernment about what details of your life you share with them (Proverbs 20:19).

> The forgiveness Christ extends to us is the pattern for the forgiveness we are to extend to others when they hurt us.

Proverbs 24:25 states, "To those who rebuke the wicked will be delight, and a good blessing will come upon them." You may need to expose and combat the sin of gossip through reproof.

Finally, Ephesians 4:32 says, "Be kind to one another, tenderhearted, forgiving each other, just as God in Christ also has forgiven you." Christ forgave our mountain of sins against Him. The forgiveness He extends to us is the pattern for the forgiveness we are to extend to others when they hurt us. You may find this difficult to do, but it's vital if you want to continue to enjoy uninterrupted fellowship with the Lord.

Why Is a Nice Girl Like You Saying Things Like That?

I did it. I engaged in gossip. It was such a mean thing to do. I was chatting with a friend who was probing into areas of my life I didn't want to discuss, so rather than reveal my true spiritual state (which obviously wasn't doing that well) I diverted the conversation by casually mentioning a "concern" I had about a mutual friend. My carefully nuanced statements about our friend took the heat off me, and that was that—or so I thought. Unbeknownst to me, my perceptive friend followed up on my "concerns" by going directly to our mutual friend to help out. Oh my, what hurt and confusion was caused by my gossip! Even now, many years later, the humiliation and shame I feel whenever I remember my behavior is enough to make me renew my vow to never gossip again.

Yet even when we know how bad slander is, how hurtful it can be, and how we have suffered from remorse over slandering others, we still find ourselves tempted to engage in it. Why? The answer is rooted in our own sinful hearts, as Jeremiah 17:9 attests: "The heart is more deceitful than all else and is desperately sick; who can understand it?" Even with the Holy Spirit residing in us, we still battle our flesh, which shows up all too frequently in our speech as gossip, slander, or unkind words.

James understands this battle all too well as he discusses that powerful and destructive little organ in our mouths called the tongue (James 3:2-10). He explains that we all stumble in our speech, and in fact, he says only the *perfect* (or mature) man is able to control his tongue completely. So where does that leave the rest of us? Obviously, we are not perfect yet, but we can learn to control our speech little by little, day by day, so it will be said of us as it was of the Proverbs 31 woman: "She opens her mouth in wisdom, and the teaching of kindness is on her tongue" (Proverbs 31:26).

"Putting On" a Different Way of Speaking

It's not okay to maintain ungodly speech. The Bible makes it clear in Romans 1:28-32 that those who make a habit of gossiping and slandering others actually hate God. We don't want to bring shame upon the name of Christ by speaking like unbelievers. That is why it's important we understand the negative impact our speech can have. Gossip fits into a special category labeled by Paul as the "deeds of the flesh" in Galatians 5:19-21. And when we give in to unkind speech those "deeds of the flesh" are evident in our lives.

That's why believers are called to put away the "deeds of the flesh." Galatians 5:17 tells us, "The flesh sets its desire against the Spirit, and the Spirit against the flesh." The Holy Spirit resides in every believer, and opposes sinful speech. He wants to help us live according to His ways. But when we give in to the flesh we squelch the blessing of the Holy Spirit and destroy the crop of godly fruit the Holy Spirit desires to produce in our lives. This is why we are told to "crucify the flesh with its passions and desires" and to "walk by the Spirit" (Galatians 5:24-25).

Ephesians 4:31 and Colossians 3:8 tell us to put away malice, slander, bitterness, and abusive speech. From the moment of our salvation, our speech is to be characterized in new ways. Kind, gentle, patient, and edifying words are to be the norm, so it is essential that we learn how to speak in a God-honoring way.

Ground Zero for Controlling Our Tongues

The key to learning how to control our tongues is to spend less time in the flesh and more time walking in the Spirit. Galatians 5:16 assures us that when we walk by the Spirit, we "will not carry out the desire of the flesh." As we learn to apply this principle in our lives our spiritual muscles will grow stronger, and we will be less likely to give in to the temptation to gossip.

First, remember that walking by the Spirit is living *by faith*. Just as you received the Holy Spirit by faith, so walking in His power *must be* by faith as well. Ask the Lord to help your speech be pleasing to Him.

Second, remember that when we are in the flesh the Holy Spirit is not in control. He is present in every believer, but walking in the Spirit is a command, a choice we must make (Galatians 5:16). We have a choice to either obey God's Word or disregard it. If we do give in to the flesh, we must learn to quickly confess and repent of our sin. As we make it a habit to quickly repent of our sins, we "put to death" the deeds of the flesh and walk by faith in the power of the Holy Spirit.

Third, don't fool yourself. So often we want to justify words we spoke carelessly or wrongly, and we end up living in denial about our sin. If we do this we will forfeit the blessing and power of walking in the Spirit. We will be like an appliance that is plugged into the outlet yet has the power turned off.

Paul said you can tell if you are walking in the power of the Holy Spirit when the fruit of the Holy Spirit's character is seen in your life. Galatians 5:22-23 reminds us of what that fruit looks like: "The fruit of the Spirit is love, joy, peace, patience, kindness, goodness, faithfulness, gentleness, self-control; against such things there is no law."

> We can manifest as much love, joy, peace, patience, kindness, goodness, faithfulness, gentleness, and self-control as we like.

Can you have love, joy, peace, patience, kindness, *bitterness*, and goodness and still be walking in the Spirit? Or what if you replaced faithfulness, gentleness, or self-control with *gossip*? We can't lie to ourselves. The deeds of the flesh cancel out the fruit of the Spirit. It's not until we turn away from those fleshly acts and confess them to God that we can again walk by the Spirit. And if our sinful speech harms someone else, we must also go to that person and ask their forgiveness as well.

Paul concluded his list of spiritual fruit with the words "against such things there is no law." There are commands against engaging in the deeds of the flesh, but there is no law, or limit, to how much fruit of the Spirit we exhibit in our lives. Just think of it: We can manifest as much love, joy, peace, patience, kindness, goodness, faithfulness, gentleness, and self-control as we like. We don't need to hold back on this one, girls! Walking in the Spirit *always* gives glory to God and harms no one.

Finally, don't leave room in your mind to justify the sins of the tongue. We are told to "put away" and "put to death" the sins of the tongue. Paul reminds us that "those who belong to Christ Jesus have crucified the flesh with its passions and desires" (Galatians 5:24). When you consider gossip and slanderous speech dead, then you won't look for ways to resurrect them.

The Beauty of Pleasant Words

When we bought our house in Southern California, it was a dump. It had been neglected and abused for too many years. Everything needed work! It was so filthy I didn't want to touch anything. But its "bones were good," so we bought it. Through my husband's hard work and energy, our home was transformed from something "a little scary to live in" to a lovely—and clean—home. In a similar manner, God desires to transform our speech from something "scary" and sinful to something beautiful and edifying.

I don't know who coined the guidelines below, but may God bless whomever it was, for these guidelines have been a great help to me and they will surely benefit you too. Before you talk about someone else, train yourself to first consider:

Is it true?

Before you share your opinion, consider the information you wish to convey: Is it true about that person or situation? If you don't have all the facts, you should withhold your comments, or at the very least, acknowledge you don't possess all the details.

Is it kind?

The words you desire to speak may be true, but are they kind? Many people have been wounded by those who were just "telling the truth." Proverbs 3:3-4 states, "Do not let kindness and truth leave you; bind them around your neck, write them on the tablet of your heart. So you will find favor and good repute in the sight of God and man." We please the Lord when we consider how to speak the truth in a gracious way.

Is it necessary?

Ephesians 4:29 tells us we are to speak words "good for edification according to the need of the moment, so that it will give grace to those who hear." Ask yourself, "How would this information benefit the hearer?"

We will find our speech is much more likely to reflect our Lord and

Savior Jesus Christ when we filter our thoughts and words through the sieve of "Is it true?" "Is it kind?" "Is it necessary?" Yet those guidelines are only part of the process of growing more gracious in our speech. By leaning on the Lord and immersing ourselves in His Word we will find that our words will "give grace to those who hear" (Ephesians 4:29).

A Prayer for Acceptable Speech

Psalm 19:14 eloquently states the desire of every woman who longs to honor the Lord with her words: "Let the words of my mouth and the meditation of my heart be acceptable in Your sight, O LORD, my rock and my Redeemer." Now that's a prayer for our lifetime: For our words and thoughts to please the Lord because He is our rock and our Redeemer.

It always comes back to the Lord, doesn't it? Everything we do, every word that we speak, is for Him, a reflection of our delight in obeying Him and loving Him more deeply.

1. What are the effects of slander? See Psalm 31:13; Proverbs 6:19; 16:28; 25:23; and 26:20.

2. How should you respond to slander? See Psalm 34:13; Proverbs 20:19; Ephesians 4:31; Titus 3:1-2; James 4:11; and 1 Peter 2:1.

3. Unguarded speech can be overcome, but what is necessary if we are going to control our tongues? See Galatians 5:16-17,22-23; Ephesians 1:13; and Colossians 3:1-11.

4. When we are walking in the Spirit, what will our speech look like? See Ephesians 4:25-27,29,32; 5:19-20; and Colossians 3:16.

5. What do the following verses teach us about controlling our tongues? See Proverbs 16:32; 17:27-28; and 25:28.

6. When are you most tempted to engage in gossip or slander? What tools has God provided to help you overcome that temptation?

7. What are some specific ways you can speak with gracious, edifying words?

Chapter 6

The Art of Self-control

A concerned husband once confided, "When we were first married, my wife and I would occasionally drink a glass of wine to help us relax after a hectic day. At first all was fine, but eventually I noticed my wife was wanting a drink every night. It was as if she couldn't cope with the circumstances of the day unless she drank wine in the evening. When I have talked with her about this pattern, she has quit, but that never seems to last. It's not long before she resumes her pattern of drinking every night. It's gotten to the point that we even leave family gatherings early in the evening so she can get home to drink. My wife is a wonderful woman, but her drinking controls our lives." What heartache lies within his statement that "her drinking controls our lives"!

It's scenarios like this one that the apostle Paul had in mind when he addressed areas of our lives that we must govern with self-control. For a believer must exercise self-control in every area of her life, not just when it comes to drinking alcohol. That is why it is critical that we each understand the *dangers* of becoming entangled in sin and, more importantly, how to break free from sin's grip. If we are sucked into the vortex of some sin, we are unable to live out God's priorities for us. Sin's power weakens our spiritual vitality. We must learn to swim to Christ for safety. So let's take a look at how we can overcome slavery to *any* sin.

Making God's Priority of Self-control Your Priority

So far we have learned from Titus 2:3 the godly woman is to be reverent in her behavior and careful with her words. Then Paul tells us she is not to be "enslaved to much wine." For some reason this command strikes a nerve whenever it is brought up. Everyone, it seems, has an opinion about Christians and alcohol consumption, which ranges from complete teetotaling to imbibing freely. While it's recommended and commendable for believers to develop convictions about godly living, we must make sure those convictions are based upon the sure footing of God's immovable Word, and aren't just manmade rules.

To begin with, let's consider Titus 2:3, which tells us that women are not to be enslaved to much wine. Paul doesn't say women can't drink wine ever, but prohibits being *enslaved* to "much wine." He leaves room for the consumption of wine, but warns against its abuse. At this point some may say, "Aha! See, we can drink wine!" But it's vital to recognize that the *permission* to drink wine has its limit. We must remember Ephesians 5:18, which, among other texts, makes it abundantly clear that getting drunk is a sin.

As we consider this issue, we must keep in mind that in Paul's time wine was a common drink. The drink choices people had at the time were few—water, wine, or hard drink. By contrast, today we have row after row of juices, milks, coffees, or teas at the supermarket. In ancient Israel, wine was viewed as a blessing from God and a symbol of prosperity. Wine was also used for medicinal purposes—in 1 Timothy 5:23 Paul told Timothy to drink a little wine to help his stomach and ailments. In the parable of the good Samaritan, the good Samaritan used wine to help the injured man's wounds heal (Luke 10:34).

The Scriptures also record that godly people such as Melchizedek, Abraham, David, Solomon, and Daniel drank wine. And who can forget that Jesus' first recorded miracle was the turning of water into wine at the wedding feast in Cana in John 2? Now, some people have argued that the wine they drank back then was usually severely diluted with water. At certain times it was, but usually not. Yet whether the wine was diluted or not, virtually everyone in Bible times drank wine. It was the *overconsumption* of wine that the Bible warned against.

The Dangers of Drunkenness

Noah got drunk and uncovered himself before his sons, which lead to Ham being cursed for looking upon Noah's nakedness (Genesis 9:20-22). Later in Genesis, Lot got drunk twice and in each instance committed incest with his daughters (Genesis 19:32-35). It would be nice if situations like that happened only rarely when people got drunk, but they don't. Foolish and wicked behavior is *always* associated with drunkenness. Proverbs 20:1 points out, "Wine is a mocker, strong drink a brawler, and whoever is intoxicated by it is not wise." Drunkenness leads to a general lack of wisdom, to contention, and to a contemptuous spirit. Proverbs 23:20-21 adds poverty and laziness to the already-long list of consequences caused by drunkenness.

That's why, in regard to wine, God placed restrictions on those who were leaders. Proverbs 31:4-5 states, "It is not for kings to drink wine, or for rulers to desire strong drink, for they will drink and forget what is decreed, and pervert the rights of all the afflicted." It is not wise, the Bible says, when those who are entrusted with leadership drink wine, for it will cause them to forget the needs of their people and to pervert justice.

Drunkenness is also associated with the deeds of darkness (Romans 13:12-13), the deeds of the flesh (Galatians 5:19-21), and the behavior of unbelievers (1 Peter 4:3-4). Not only does Scripture provide anecdotal stories illustrating the foolishness of drunken behavior, but most importantly, believers are commanded *to not get drunk* with wine (Ephesians 5:18). This doesn't provide a loophole that allows us to get drunk with *other* alcoholic beverages. But it does furnish us with the principle that *any* substance that can hinder wise judgment is to be avoided. The bottom line for every believer is that drunkenness of any kind is sin.

Daring to Play on the Edge of the Cliff

Yet even with such clearly stated commands in the Bible there are some, wanting to use their liberties, who ask where the "edge of the cliff" is so they can drink and yet not get drunk. That is an impossible question to answer. Drunkenness begins at a different point for each person. The only way to discover the cliff's edge is by getting drunk and falling off the edge. Yet we can't do that because we are commanded to not get drunk *under any circumstances*. If we endeavor to determine at what point drunkenness occurs, we cross over into sin.

Worse yet is what the "At what point do I cross the line?" mindset reveals about the heart. The question "How close can I get to danger before falling into sin?" is the wrong one to ask. The wise person asks, "Where can I stand so I never fall off the cliff?" Those who are wise understand the dangers of even standing near the "line" and seek to stay well back from the danger. They will never be in peril of falling off the edge of the cliff.

What Are You Mastered By?

Understanding the dangers of playing near the edge of the cliff is helpful when trying to avoid any sin. The word "enslaved" in Titus 2:3 means "to make a slave of, to come under bondage, to be subservient to."[1] If we become "enslaved" to much wine, wine actually becomes our master, and we become its slave. If we are not governed by self-control, wine can end up governing our lives. We end up doing its bidding because we are its slaves. Because wine is a patient tyrant, it enslaves us by degrees until we are owned and ruled by this mercurial and cruel master.

And alcohol isn't the only thing to which we can become enslaved. Titus 3:3 tells us we can become enslaved to "various lusts and pleasures" as well. Even things that aren't inherently sinful, such as food, can enslave us if we don't use self-control. Once something becomes our master, then it also becomes sin to us. Susanna Wesley once wrote, "Whatever weakens your reason, impairs the tenderness of your conscience, obscures your sense of God, or takes off the relish of spiritual things; in short, whatever increases the strength and authority of your body over your mind—that thing is sin to you, however innocent it may be in itself."[2] These wise words shed light on the dangers that *anything* in our lives can pose if we are overcome by them.

As believers, we are to live as the slaves of Christ. Christ is our Lord and Master, and we are to line ourselves up with Him and His ways. Never is a believer to serve two masters. When we become enslaved to anything other than Christ and His righteousness we are trying to do the impossible—serve two masters. A slave who tries to serve two masters will end up despising one and being devoted to the other (Matthew 6:24). Therefore, we must make sure that Christ is our *only* Master.

Prior to coming to know the Lord Jesus Christ as our Savior, we had no choice but to serve our wicked and despotic master, Satan. Yet Christ, in His great power and love, broke the chains of sin and slavery to Satan so we could be free to serve a new Master. Romans 6:17-18 triumphantly proclaims, "Thanks be to God that though *you were slaves of sin*, you became obedient from the heart to that form of teaching to which you were committed, and *having been freed from sin, you became slaves of righteousness.*"

Paul was saying that believers have been freed to serve Christ. But, as any Christian will tell you, we often choose to return to our old master and put on his chains of slavery again. This idea is summed up in Galatians 5:1, where Paul reminds us, "It was for freedom that Christ set us free; therefore keep standing firm and do not be subject again to a yoke of slavery."

I remember when, as a young believer, the first time I heard and understood what it meant to be free from slavery to sin and Satan. I had been struggling to overcome certain sins from my old way of life, but felt defeated and hopeless. When I shared this with an older brother in the Lord, he read Galatians 5:1 to me. The proverbial "lightbulb" turned on in my head: Christ had set me free! The promise of Scripture gave me the power to overcome those sins that had so often been a snare to me in the past. I was no longer Satan's slave, and my new Master would enable me to walk in His ways. Hope sprang forth in my heart. I wouldn't have to live in defeat any longer!

Like a Dog on a Chain

My husband often illustrates our presalvation slavery to sin by comparing us to a dog tied to a stake in the middle of a large yard. As unbelievers, we were like a dog chained to sin. Our freedom to move about the yard never extended outside the circle of sin. Though there are many ways we can move about the yard, we can only move within the sphere of sin. We can never escape that sphere, which makes it impossible for us to please God.

Then when we turn to Christ in faith and repent of our sins, Christ breaks the chain that kept us in bondage to sin. Just like a dog that is let loose after being chained up all day, so we are free to run to our new Master. Yet also like a dog let off its chain, we often return to the circle of sin. We have spent so much time tied up there in the past that we developed hard-to-break sinful habits. We find it easier to continue engaging in those sinful practices than to enjoy the freedom and new life available to us in Christ.

> The good news for us is that no matter how the slavery
> began, the path to freedom is the same for every sin.

No Longer Chained to Sin

Because we are no longer slaves to sin, we are to live like a free person, no longer in bondage to sin and its entanglements. And this applies not only to wine or alcohol, but to anything that can enslave us, take our heart and mind away from Christ, or cause us to sin. We are to use self-control and stay clear of anything that can master us. As 2 Peter 2:19 clearly states, "By what a man is overcome, by this he is enslaved."

Even though as Christians we have been freed from sin's tyranny, Titus 2:3 warns us against being enslaved to it. When we give in to temptation, we become a voluntary slave of sin's grip and power. We are owned by it. And the struggle to avoid slavery to sin is a lifelong effort.

Are You Enslaved and Unaware of It?

You may find yourself thinking, *This is silly. I am not enslaved to any sin. I don't think any sin has its hold on me!* And perhaps you are absolutely right in your assessment. Yet enslavement to sin is a funny thing.

Often the very area in which we are most adamant that we *don't* have a problem is the very area in which we do. It is also possible to initially participate in an activity that is not sinful yet become enslaved to it over time. Once enslaved, that activity can, in turn, lead to other sins in our lives. After we become a slave of one sin, we can end up adding sin upon sin. Thomas Watson, a Puritan from the English Reformation, wrote about this truth: "One sin will make way for more, as a little thief can open the door to more. Sins are linked and chained together. One sin will draw on more. David's adultery made way for murder. One sin never goes alone."[3] The good news for us is that no matter how the slavery began, *the path to freedom is the same* for every sin.

Let's consider an example of how we are tricked into becoming slaves of sin, and what we can do when we find ourselves enslaved. There are certain sites on the Internet that are great for connecting with family and friends. Used in moderation, such sites are beneficial and fun. Yet it's possible to become addicted to checking on such sites continually to the point we neglect life's priorities. We become so ensnared at seeing what's new that we become idle busybodies. What began as a simple way to interact with friends and family ends up distracting and enslaving us.

We can become enslaved by food. In and of itself, food is not sinful. We all have to eat. But what, when, and how much we eat can become enslaving. If you find you are engaging in certain kinds of eating habits that are bearing unhealthy consequences or place too much emphasis on food, then food has become your master.

Even certain kinds of thoughts or emotions, ranging from pity parties to immorality, can enslave us. Worry, fear, anxiety, and fretting are common sins that enslave many women. Once enslaved, these sinful emotions and thoughts can steal our joy, zap our spiritual vitality, quench the Spirit, and prevent us from giving glory to God.

How to Tell If You Are Enslaved

Below are four questions we can use to examine our hearts to see if we are enslaved to sin in a particular area. You can use these questions as a "diagnostic tool" to assess your heart and spiritual life.

- Do you feel defensive when someone asks you about a particular area of your life? Why do you think you feel defensive?

- Do you make excuses about why you are engaging in a particular activity? Why do you feel the need to make excuses?

- Do you minimize the amount of time you spend on that area?

- Do you try to hide that activity from others?

Thomas Watson described the sin that enslaves us as our "beloved or besetting" sin. He said, "The sin which a man does not love to have reproved is the darling sin." And, "There is usually one sin that is the favorite, the sin which the heart is most fond of. A beloved sin lies in a man's bosom as the disciple whom Jesus loved leaned on His bosom."[4]

Overcoming the Entanglements of Sin

When you answered the questions above, did you discover red flags? Sometimes we become enslaved so subtly that we don't realize what has happened. That is why we must make it a habit to consistently evaluate our spiritual lives, looking for weak spots and areas of sin. Just because you check to see if your child has a dirty diaper and the diaper proves to be clean doesn't mean you should never check it again. You must keep checking the diaper because sooner or later it will get dirty. Likewise, we need to examine our hearts continually. And when we discover a problem area, we can begin to target it with prayer, confession, repentance, and the Word of God. These things will equip us to hack through the entangling undergrowth of those sins that have wrapped their thorny and clinging vines around us. Battling sin is a constant struggle in the Christian life.

As we interact with God's Word, it strengthens and changes us so that we can experience increasing victory over the lusts of the flesh.

When we find ourselves enslaved to sin, we must begin breaking free by seeking the Lord's help. We came to Christ by faith, and we must continue to live by faith, asking the Lord for help in overcoming our sin and leaning on Him for assistance in the fight. We must remember we have been given a new nature and all-sufficient grace to overcome sin and the desires of the flesh. Our greatest ally against sin is the Word of God. Psalm 119:11 reminds us of this truth: "Your Word I have treasured in my heart, that I may not sin against You." The transforming power of God's Word changes us from the inside out. As we interact with God's Word, it strengthens and changes us so that we can experience increasing victory over the lusts of the flesh.

The Steps to Self-control

The terms *enslaved* and *addicted* indicate a voluntary alliance with or a mastery of our will by something or someone other than God. Perhaps you don't drink too much wine, but you may find you're in bondage to food, certain kinds of books, smoking, impure thoughts, sexual sin, television, movies, surfing the Internet, gossip...the list could go on and on! Whatever the case, as Christians, our master is Christ alone. This means saying yes to Christ and no to the things that distract or enslave us. We need to exercise self-control and stand far back from the edge of the cliff.

Because every believer receives the Holy Spirit at salvation, he or she will exhibit the qualities of the Holy Spirit as they grow in their Christian life. Self-control is one of those qualities. Self-control must govern our speech, our drinking and eating, how we dress, our finances, and yes, even our emotions. Self-control is what sets Christians apart from the rest of the world. Living self-controlled lives makes us effective witnesses for Christ. This is why we must practice self-control—it demonstrates to the world we are followers of Christ.

What if *today* you said no to that area which entangles you? What if you said no to that area again tomorrow, and the day after that, and the day after that? How would your life be affected by the discipline of overcoming self? God will help you win this battle if you ask Him. Lean on Him for strength, guidance, and wisdom by using the resources He has put at your disposal.

If you find something other than Christ is your master, and it has you in its grip, then you need to begin to break those bonds with the ax of repentance and the bolt cutter of confession. Try writing down what is entangling you. Then list what sins have resulted from indulging in that area of entanglement. Often one sin, if left unchecked, can lead to a host of sins that wreak havoc with your walk with the Lord. In addition to confessing these sins and repenting of them, it's wise for you to share your struggles with a mature believer who will faithfully pray for you and hold you accountable as you take steps to overcome your sin. Also, study the Bible to discover what it says about overcoming your particular kind of entanglement, and draft a plan of attack for overcoming it. Make sure your plan includes ways to *put off, lay aside, flee from,* and *avoid* this entanglement, as well as positive ways to *replace* your sin so that your life will honor the Lord.

We are to give all our allegiance and love to God. We are to make Him our all in all and give our hearts completely to Him. Amazing as it seems, exercising self-control in our lives—a self-control motivated by our love for God—reflects the devotion and gratitude we have toward Him. May the Lord give us the grace and courage to overcome anything in our lives that takes our eyes off Him.

1. God's Word warns that we not become enslaved by much wine. What attitudes and behaviors are associated with drunkenness? See Romans 13:12-13; Galatians 5:19,21; Ephesians 5:15-18; Philippians 3:18-19; and 1 Peter 4:3-4.

2. What are some reasons the Bible gives for exercising self-control when it comes to drinking alcohol? See Proverbs 20:1; 23:20-21,29-35; Ephesians 5:18; and 1 Peter 4:3-5.

3. What principles about self-control can you extract from the following verses? See Proverbs 25:16; Romans 13:14; 14:13-23; Galatians 5:22-24; and 2 Peter 1:4-11.

4. Define "enslaved" in Titus 2:3. What kinds of things can a person become enslaved to?

5. By their very definition the terms *enslaved* and *addicted* indicate an alliance with something or someone other than God. Is there anything in your life to which you are enslaved? What basic steps must you take to *break* those

entanglements? Read Psalms 32:1-11; 66:18; Hebrews 12:12-13; and 1 John 1:9.

6. In what areas of your life do you battle using self-control? What steps must you take to exercise self-control with greater success?

7. Finally, write down at least one verse from this study that will help and encourage you to master self-control.

Chapter 7

The Art of
Sharing and Seeking Wisdom

og descended upon the mountain, making the drive home after a day of skiing a treacherous journey. Car after car slowly inched its way down the steep inclines and around the hairpin curves. Straining to see the road in front of them, drivers searched for glimpses of the yellow line painted at the center of the road, or the white line on the shoulder, which separated them from the mountain's perilous edge. All that was familiar had been swallowed up in the dense fog, and only the faint taillights of the cars in front guided the drivers in the now heavily shrouded surroundings. Like children on a field trip who are admonished by their teacher to join hands so they won't get lost, each car in the band cautiously followed the car in front of them until they made it down the mountain to safety. How thankful all the drivers were for the person immediately in front who showed the way down the mountain, each one relying upon the one who preceded them!

God's plan for the Christian life is similar. It involves the close following of another's "light" while we continue our journey to the heavenly city. Ever since Jesus trained the Twelve and commissioned them to make disciples, teaching them all that Jesus commanded (Matthew 28:19-20), there has been an unbroken string of lights through the ages, teachers who have helped others to make their way through the dense fog of this world. It is what Paul spoke of in 2 Timothy 2:2 when he said, "The things which you have heard from me in the presence of many witnesses, entrust these to faithful men who will be able to teach others also." How you and I proceed on life's road affects those who come behind us. They depend upon us to lead them in the right way. It is for this reason that, in Titus 2:3, the older women are admonished to make it a priority to be "teaching what is good" to those who follow them.

The phrase "teaching what is good" is one word in the original Greek text, and is used only once in the New Testament, here in Titus 2:3. It is a compound of two words, *didaskalos*, meaning "teacher," and *kalos*, which means "good," from which the phrase is translated "teaching what is good" or "teacher of good things."[1]

A teacher is one who instructs, trains, tutors, and educates, yet teaching is not limited to the imparting of knowledge only, but the example of the teacher's life as well. A *good* teacher is a means of change and growth for those she teaches as she imparts her knowledge and life skills. Titus 2:3 makes it clear that every woman is to pass on to other women the who, what, when, why, and how of God's priorities for us.

The Good Things We Are to Pass On to Others

God's priorities for women are good things. The phrase "teaching what is good" is similar to the phrase "reverent behavior," which we studied earlier. Both *reverent behavior* and *teaching what is good* undergird the priorities a godly woman pursues to impact the lives of others. To teach what is good is to convey all that is honorable, right, and noble about being a Christian woman. It is to impart the joys and duties of God's calling for every woman and to equip the next generation for that same high calling. Of course, all this information is found in God's Word, which we must first learn and practice before we can impart it to others.

Though "teaching what is good" is a broad term, we can catch detailed glimpses of what it means by looking at Titus 2:3-5. A Christian woman who desires to honor the Lord will bring each area of her life under the umbrella of "good things." The teacher of good things is to share with others the lessons she has learned about self-control and the entanglements of sin, and the day-to-day attitudes and skills necessary for taking care of our families and homes, all while modeling godly behavior. That is what it means to teach others "what is good."

We gain further insight into what it means to teach what is good when we eavesdrop on Samuel speaking to the people of Israel after they requested a human king, just like the other nations had. Samuel responded by saying, "Far be it from me that I should sin against the LORD by ceasing to pray for you; but *I will instruct you in the good and right way.*" We need instruction that will put us on the good path. Solomon used similar terminology when he prayed for the Israelites at the dedication of the temple and asked the Lord to teach them "the good way in which they should walk" (1 Kings 8:36). Teaching what is good flows out of a life that walks in the good and right way that is pleasing to the Lord.

By contrast, those who do not walk in God's ways listen to their own counsel and follow what *they* think is right, according to Isaiah 65:2. Clearly, those who teach good things live in a way that matches their instruction. If we don't follow God's ways, then we have no "right" to teach what is good.

Who We Are to Teach

We see in the Scriptures examples of godly women who taught other women or their children. Naomi guided Ruth when they returned to Bethlehem as two widows. Hannah trained Samuel before taking him up to the tabernacle to serve Eli. Solomon eloquently referred to the benefit he received from his mother's teaching and in Proverbs 1:8 urged others not to forsake their mother's teaching. Paul alluded to the teaching Timothy received from his godly mother, Eunice, and grandmother, Lois, as the means God used to bring Timothy to faith as a young boy.

Paul exhorted the Thessalonian believers, saying, "We urge you, brethren, admonish the unruly, encourage the fainthearted, help the weak, be patient with everyone" (1 Thessalonians 5:14). This verse reveals we are to teach whoever comes across our path, whether they fit into the category of "unruly," "fainthearted," or "weak." Our purpose in teaching what is good is to build up and encourage others to live according to God's priorities.

The Scriptures also provide insight into who we are—or rather, who we are *not*—supposed to teach. Both 1 Corinthians 14:34-35 and 1 Timothy 2:8-15 unequivocally state women are *not* "to teach or exercise spiritual authority" over men (1 Timothy 2:12). In both passages the apostle Paul addressed God's role for women in the church.[2] Just as Christ is the head of the church, so husbands are the leaders in the home and the church. This is God's perfect plan for men and women. And every woman who desires to live by God's priorities will seek to function within the parameters He has given her in the church and home. When we teach and model God's priorities in the way He designed, we are communicating to others the good things God desires women to know and understand.

Learning How to Study God's Word

God, in His Word, has clearly communicated His will for us, leaving a well-marked path for us to follow. Every priority He wants us to know about is contained within the pages of the Bible. God didn't leave anything out. The Bible contains everything we need for life and godliness (2 Peter 1:3).

Some women have disregarded God's priorities for them. When they do this, they are in effect saying, "*We* know what is best for our homes and the church, not God." If we pick and choose the parts of God's Word we want to obey, and disregard the parts we don't like, we place ourselves over God. By contrast, when we acknowledge God's Word as true, accurate, and applicable for today, we declare His right to rule over us as our Lord and King.

Because the Bible is God's will recorded for us, we don't have to wonder how to please Him or figure out what is important to Him. Every believer needs to learn to study and interpret God's Word correctly. We must learn to live by *what God says* rather than what we think is best. And by adhering to some simple rules for effective Bible study, we can learn to correctly apply God's Word to our lives. Here are a few simple steps to get you started.

CONSIDER THE CONTEXT

The first, and most important, rule of Bible study is to remember the *context* of the passage reigns as king over any problems or questions that may surface. Often people will read a verse and try to understand it without taking into consideration the details that come both before and after it. Doing that is like going to the middle of a ten-page letter, reading a sentence on page five, and assuming you can understand that one sentence completely without knowing the details that came before and after it. When we take time to understand how a verse fits in with the rest of the chapter or book, then we are better able to glean its meaning.

Observe the Passage

The next rule of Bible study is to simply observe what the passage is saying. By carefully reading the verse or passage within its context you will gain insight into what it says. Resist the urge to leap ahead to application. Trying to see "what it means to me" before understanding "what the passage says" is like trying a new recipe without reading the directions all the way through before you begin.

Determine the Meaning

The next step in Bible study is to ask, "What did the original audience understand this passage to mean?" Answering this question before you attempt to apply the passage will help protect you from misunderstanding it. Seek to find out what the *original audience* understood the *original author* to mean by what he wrote.

Discover the Application

Finally, you can ask, "What timeless principles, truths, or facts about God, Christ, or man apply to me from this text?" And, "How can I put them into practice in my life?"

These basic steps will get you started on a life-changing journey. You will learn to nourish your soul, and in turn, become a skilled chef of God's truth who can impart soul nourishment to others. You can learn to study and accurately handle God's Word, and when you do, you will be well on your way to being a faithful student of God's Word who is able to teach what is good.

Everyone Is Called to Teach

Each of us possesses the ability to teach others in some way or another, or God would never have commanded us to do so in Titus 2:3. Some may have the gift of teaching and lead a women's Bible study or teach the Bible in children's church. Others may not have the gift of teaching, yet we are all called to teach in some way. We can teach others by sharing the gospel with unbelievers, we can teach as we train our children in God's ways, and we can teach through discipleship and our example. If we remember that teaching can encompass everything from formal classroom instruction to the gentle conversations we have while preparing dinner, we can begin to understand that each one of us is called to serve as a teacher in one way or another.

The Method of Our Teaching

In Deuteronomy 6:7 we find God's instructions to the people of Israel: "You shall teach [My commands] diligently to your sons and shall talk of them when you sit in your house and when you walk by the way and when you lie down and when you rise up." Deuteronomy 6:7 models how we can use every opportunity to teach others good things. As we go about our day, we are to teach others in the ways that are good according to God's Word—through little conversations, gentle words of instruction, and wise counsel.

> The goal of our teaching is to produce wisdom
> and righteousness in those we teach.

Even now you may find yourself thinking, *But I'm no teacher!* Perhaps the idea of teaching someone *anything* is terrifying to you and makes you shiver at the thought, and yet we are all told to teach what is good. Be encouraged! When God tells you to do something, you can rest assured He will also help you to obey Him. He will equip you and help you to follow Him as you use the gifts He has given you. And because each of us is gifted in different ways, what you teach and how you pass those things on to others will look very different from what and how your friend teaches. So don't grow fainthearted. Remember, God does not make mistakes! He will use you to strengthen the faith of others if you will step out in faith and teach.

The Goal of Our Teaching

Whether we think we can teach or not, it is God's plan for us to model and teach what is good. Galatians 6:10 urges us, "While we have opportunity, let us do good to all people, and especially to those who are of the household of the faith." We have no idea how long we will have to "do good" to those around us, so we must take the opportunities while they are given. Proverbs 14:22 speaks with favor about those who "devise good." Think about the difference it would make in our lives, homes, churches, and hearts if each one of us "devised good" by pouring our energies and resources into being teachers of good to one another!

The goal of our teaching is to produce wisdom and righteousness in those we teach. In Proverbs 4:11 Solomon wrote to his son, "I have directed you in the way of wisdom; I have led you in upright paths." Proverbs 22:19-21 reveals that teaching is to help others trust the Lord more and to make them certain about His Word. When we teach not just to impart knowledge but for the purpose of equipping and training others to trust the Lord and His Word, then we will fulfill God's call in Titus 2:3 to teach "what is good."

The Scriptures help us learn what good things we are to teach by providing examples of what we are *not* to teach. For example, Colossians 2:20-23 warns against teaching legalistic, man-made rules to promote a false holiness. Anything that teaches others to rely on themselves, their emotions, their own piety, or man-made religion is not good. It distracts them from keeping their eyes on Christ, who alone is to be the object of worship.

In 1 Timothy 4:7 we are admonished to "have nothing to do with worldly fables fit only for old women." We should never use our "ministering to one another" as a way to gossip and get out of doing our housework (1 Timothy 5:13). Rumors and myths, which go down easily like dainty morsels, have no ability to nourish other people's hearts and lives. And engaging in controversies and disputes has no eternal value whatsoever. At best, these things are distractions, at their worst they distract us and others from Christ and damage our relationship with Him.

Being Teachable

As a young teacher, I was amazed to discover what terrible "students" many teachers are. They are so used to teaching others that they aren't willing to receive instruction from someone else. Being teachable is a critical part of being a teacher of what is good. So it is essential that we possess a teachable spirit at the same time that we teach others.

Here are a number of characteristics of a teachable spirit:

A Teacher of Good Listens and Accepts

Psalm 32:8-9 warns us not to be like the "horse or as the mule which have no understanding, whose trappings include bit and bridle to hold them in check, otherwise they will not come near to you." To be like a horse or mule is to be stubborn, independent, and proud, fighting instruction rather than submitting to wise counsel. Thinking or acting like you know everything reflects an unteachable spirit. Those who teach good *do not fight against* helpful instruction; instead, they maintain the attitude of a student so they can continue to learn and grow in living out God's truth.

You may feel you are teachable and that you listen to others. You may feel you do not *fight* against the helpful hints given to you, but do you *accept* them? A teachable person *receives* wise counsel and instruction, as stated in Proverbs 10:8: "The wise of heart will receive commands, but a babbling fool will be ruined." When someone tries to give you instruction or counsel, how do you receive it? Do you keep talking, get angry, try to defend yourself, or do you listen? Only a fool thinks his way is the only right way (Proverbs 12:15). A teacher of good *listens to and accepts instruction.*

A Teacher of Good Is Respectful

A teacher of good things loves and respects God's Word. Those who are teachable recognize the Scriptures contain God's will for them. They listen to His Word rather than despising it, as Proverbs 13:13 says: "The one who despises the word will be in debt to it, but the one who fears the commandment will be rewarded." How do you respond to God's Word? A teacher of good *respects* God's Word and desires to obey it.

A Teacher of Good Heeds Reproof

A teachable person understands the blessings that come from reproof. When we listen to the admonishments of friends, loved ones, and the Word of God, we gain understanding and insight. We grow wise, as Proverbs 15:31-32 states: "He whose ear listens to the life-giving reproof will dwell among the wise. He who neglects discipline despises himself, but he who listens to reproof acquires understanding." Are you able to listen to reproof without taking offense? Are you thankful for those reproving words when they are spoken to you for good? A teacher of good *heeds* reproof.

A Teacher of Good Is Humble

Those who are teachable are also humble. They understand they don't have all the answers and receive the instruction given to them (Psalm 25:9). Humility is necessary to receiving, hearing, and applying God's Word. Resisting instruction means pride, while receiving instruction means humility. Which way characterizes your response to instruction—resisting or receiving? A teacher of good is *humble*.

Being a Model of What Is Good

We are all to teach what is good. We are all to remain teachable. And we must *model* what is good. Our lives must back up what we teach if others are going to heed our instruction, especially when it comes to teaching and guiding others in the ways of life. Paul urged Titus and other young men to "show yourself to be an example of good deeds" in all things (Titus 2:7). Jesus told the disciples to follow His example after He washed their feet (John 13:15). First Timothy 4:12 explains that every area of our life—words, actions, and moral conduct—is to serve as a model for others: "Let no one look down on your youthfulness, but rather in *speech, conduct, love, faith and purity, show yourself an example* of those who believe."

Over and over again I have seen God lift up certain people as an example for others to emulate. They have made the Lord their focus and have sought to please Him in every way. As they do so, others notice their godly pursuits and begin to follow their example. The key to becoming a model for others to follow is to pursue the Lord wholeheartedly. With our eyes on Him, we show ourselves as examples in our "speech, conduct, love, faith and purity."

> Watch the lives of godly women. Listen to
> their words. Observe their choices.

Another key to becoming an example for others is to pay attention to the details of our lives. By making it a regular habit to examine our hearts and deeds, we are taking the steps necessary to overcome areas of weakness or failure. In Psalm 119:59 the psalmist tells us how to do this, saying, "I considered my ways and turned my feet to Your testimonies." When we consider our ways and assess how they line up with God's Word, we will discover any areas that may bring dishonor to the Lord. Consider your ways. What do you need to work on so your life will match your words?

Learning from Others Who Model What Is Good

I have benefitted greatly from the godly examples of other women around me. From some I have received direct instruction and help, while from others I have learned by their example and tried to emulate what they do. Through their training and example I have learned how to clean a house quickly and efficiently, to persevere in the training of my children, and how to make my husband a priority—and that's just for starters! Other women have modeled for me how to have self-control over one's emotions, how to have a worshipful quiet time, and how to have a vibrant prayer life. By interacting with, observing, and learning from the examples of other women, I have gained many insights into the Christian life. I have learned about God's sovereignty and how to persist with grace in the midst of difficulty. Their examples have been invaluable to me over the years and have helped me to grow in my walk with Christ.

Watch the lives of godly women. Listen to their words. Observe their choices. Notice the things they do and don't do. Let them serve as your teachers and observe them living out God's priorities. And just as they can help you to grow in your walk with the Lord, so God intends for you to help others as they tread along the path toward heaven.

Are You Teaching What Is Good?

We've looked at being a teacher of what is good from all angles. It is one of God's priorities for us. We show our love for God, and for others, by obeying this command from Titus 2:3. We've received instruction about what is good, we've been encouraged to serve as an example for others, and now it is time to implement what we've learned. Are you presently sharing what is good with someone else, whether younger or older? If not, what is holding you back?

Perhaps you are saying to yourself, *I don't know where or how to begin with a task like this one.* An easy way to get started is to simply spend time with other women. Attend a Bible study or serve in a ministry, and God-focused friendships will naturally form through the mutual interests of the Word and service. And out of those friendships will flow your "teaching what is good" ministry.

No matter what your age or your life situation, God has called *you* as an example of faith in God, to model love toward Christ and to live steadfastly in hope. Though the fog of unbelief and worldly distraction may cover much of the road, you are the blinking taillights of the car in front showing those who trail you how to live out God's priorities. Your faithful example gives courage and hope to those traveling the same road toward heaven as they watch you make progress in God's good ways.

Charles Spurgeon said, "A man of devotion is always a man of desires; the best people are fullest of longings to be better."[3] This is the road you travel—to do your best, to lean on the Lord, and to desire more of His grace along the way. Oh, may the Lord fulfill every desire for goodness in you and strengthen you to carry out this high calling! And may others see those good things in your life as you seek to pass them on.

1. Women are to teach what is good to one another. What good things are we called to teach, according to Titus 2:3-5?

2. What are some ways you can impart the priorities and goals of the Christian life to others? See Deuteronomy 6:7,20; Proverbs 22:17-21; 1 Thessalonians 5:14; 1 Timothy 4:12-13; and 1 Peter 5:3.

3. Of course, in order to teach what is good to others you need to model those good things to others. Second Corinthians 13:5 urges us to examine ourselves so we can align ourselves with God's Word. What do you need to work on so your life will match your words?

4. How have other women taught you good things? How has their example had an impact on your life?

5. What are some specific ways *you* can share with others the good things you know? Be realistic as you take into account your personality and life situation.

6. What are some ways you can avail yourself of good teaching at church?

Chapter 8

The Art of Loving Your Husband

She came out of the grocery store to find a single red rose held securely in place by the windshield wipers of her car. A smile of delight lit up her face as she gently lifted the rose from its position. It was pink—her favorite. She looked about the parking lot for a familiar face, but saw no one. Puzzled and a little embarrassed, she smiled to herself as she opened the car door—and there on the driver's seat was another pink rose waiting for her. She put her groceries into the car and drove home smiling and wondering about the flowered surprise.

Another flower waited for her in the entry of her home, another stood by the kitchen sink, another waited by her chair in the living room, another in the bedroom, and another on the bathroom vanity. Everywhere she looked single roses stood silently, waiting, harbingers of some surprise still to come.

She heard the front door open. *He* walked in. She hurried to the entryway and threw her arms around his neck before he even had a chance to take off his coat.

"Thank you for the flowers! They are beautiful! They're everywhere! What is happening?"

He hugged her close, then drew away slightly so he could gently cup her face in his hands. He tenderly kissed her wrinkled cheeks and said, "Honey, I want you to know that you are still my girl even after all these years of marriage. Each rose represents one of the ways you serve me and love me. It is an inadequate way to say thank you for making me a priority and loving me so faithfully."

Then he reached for her hand and gently held it in his own as he placed it over his heart while he recited Proverbs 31:11-12: "The heart of her husband trusts in her, and he will have no lack of gain. She does him good and not evil all the days of her life."

She drew in a breath and her eyes grew wide before she responded in the age-old way of women—she cried, then she laughed, then she kissed him, and then she cried some more.

Sappy story? Yes. But it illustrates the next priority God lists for us women in Titus 2:3-5. God desires women to love their husbands with the diligence and purposefulness we have applied to all of the other priorities we have looked at thus far. We spent a great deal of time in chapter 2 delving into the focused and serious mindset God desires every woman to have toward His priorities. That mindset reminds us we are to give serious consideration to the task of loving our husbands!

In fact, Titus 2:4 says we are to be *trained* in loving our husbands. Don't you find it interesting that God says we need to be trained to love our husbands? After all, we're women! We're the nurturers, the emotional-feely types. Women are the go-to experts at loving others! Or so we might be tempted to think. Yet God says women need to be trained to love their husbands.

Jack and I were married five years before we had children, so by the time we began having our kids I was very ready for them. I absolutely love being a mom and all aspects of the role—from those middle-of-the-night feedings in the early days to becoming the family chauffeur to preparing the children for adulthood. I so enjoy being with our kids that it is very easy for me to inadvertently put aside the special role God has given me of being a wife and loving my husband.

The Priority God Places on the Marriage Relationship

Titus 2:4 reveals the emphasis God places upon a woman loving her husband, but that is not the first place we learn of its importance. The book of Genesis reveals the priority God places upon the marriage relationship. When God created Adam and Eve, He declared His creation good, and that everything was as it should be. They were the first family, and that first family was complete with the two of them. Later children were added, and their family grew, but the significance of that first created relationship of husband and wife must not be lost on us today.

> If you want to raise healthy, well-adjusted
> kids, then love your husband.

Perhaps you've never thought of it this way before, but your family is complete when you get married. You and your husband constitute a family whether God blesses you with children or not. And *children are a great blessing* to the family, yet your relationship with your children must never supplant or detract from your relationship with your husband. If you want to raise healthy, well-adjusted kids, then love your husband. The security that children receive from knowing mom and dad are happy and are devoted to staying married will see them through the difficulties of growing up in a culture that no longer seems to value commitment in marriage.

Your Marriage Is a Priority Even When You Have Children

The necessity of making our marriage relationship a priority doesn't change when children enter the picture. We can't quit focusing on our relationship with our husbands though we now have "little people" to pay attention to in the family. It is often a challenge to find the time or energy to focus on the marriage relationship when children come along, but it is God's desire that we continue to do so. That is why He commands the older women to train the younger women to love their husbands.

When Leah, who is our oldest, was about three weeks old, Jack asked me to go on a date with him—just for an hour or so. Though I found leaving Leah with a loving babysitter extremely difficult for even that short period of time, I knew what he was doing was right. He knew we needed to establish—from the very beginning—the priority of our marriage relationship, even over that of being parents. Finding time to be together as a couple grew more difficult as more children came along. Finding a babysitter, navigating through cold season, and being on a tight budget often made me want to give up, but remembering that happy marriages produce happy families made me persevere. Parenting is tough enough without adding to it the stresses of an unhappy or strained marriage.

Your Marriage Is a Priority Through All the Seasons of Life

Then when the children are almost grown or have left the nest we face another challenge. Usually by then we've been married a long time. We've settled into a routine. We know our spouse's patterns and habits. So it's easy to be lulled into complacency about our marriage and become negligent in making our husbands a priority.

That is why God commands the older women to train the younger women to love their husbands. Of course if an older woman is going to teach a younger woman about loving her husband, then it means she must have modeled the making of her husband a priority through *all* the years of her own marriage, through every season of life. I don't know what I thought marriage would look like after Jack and I had been married a long time; I guess I thought we would be so joined at the hip we would never be bothered by conflict or even have the need for making each other a priority. I thought that would happen all by itself.

But that is not the case. The command to love my husband and make him a priority is still as urgent and necessary now as it was during the first years of our marriage. There are many days when I find marriage in these middle years a *greater* challenge than I ever did in the early days. I think part of that happens because the longer we are married, the more we accumulate "baggage" that we must throw out—all while the demands upon our time, relationships, and resources increase.

After many years of marriage, you may find yourselves becoming more independent of each other rather than working as a team. The rhythm of the day-to-day routine can lull even the happiest of couples into complacency. All too often we expect our spouse to respond in predictable patterns rather than praying for them and looking for the Lord's transforming work in their character. More often than we admit, we let a little bitterness creep into our relationship, which colors how we view our "hunny-bunny dew drop." We tend to divide and conquer when it comes to doing errands, rather than doing them together as we did in the early years of our marriage. If we are to love our husband as God commands us to in Titus 2:4, then we must *continue* to make him the priority God intends him to be, even in the midst of all the commitments and duties we have come to accumulate in our middle years.

The Kind of Love We Are to Have for Our Husbands

The world thinks of love as sex, or as something ephemeral that can float in and out of one's life like the fog, or as being like getting struck by lightning. The world sees love as an emotion that compels a person to do all kinds of unusual and crazy things. Our world has many inaccurate views of love that contribute to much of the confusion that takes place in relationships.

If we aren't careful, we can inadvertently freight a worldly understanding of love into the biblical meaning of love. Titus 2:4 tells us women must love their husbands, so it's vital that we gain a clear picture of what God means when He uses the term "love." The ancient Greeks had three words to describe different kinds of love. There is *agape*, which is described as the unconditional love God exhibits toward us. There is *eros*, from which we get the word *erotic*. This describes the physical love between a husband and a wife. And then there is the word *philos*, which is used to describe the love that occurs between friends. And interestingly, it is not *agape* or *eros* the apostle Paul used in Titus 2:4 to describe the way women are to love their husbands, but *philos*.

The Beauty of Phileo Love

The Greek word *phileo* is generally summed up as the friendship kind of love. Most of us have heard of the city of Philadelphia, which is the city of "brotherly love." People sometimes dismiss *phileo* love as a lesser kind of love that does not quite attain to the nobility of *agape* love, yet nothing could be further from the truth. We see *phileo* love demonstrated in John 11:3 when Mary and Martha sent word to Jesus about their brother, Lazarus, saying, "Lord, behold, he whom You love is sick." They recognized the great affection Jesus had for their family. It was Jesus' close friendship with Lazarus that moved them to seek Jesus' help. Later, when Lazarus died from his illness, Jesus demonstrated His love for His friend by weeping for him and the sorrowing family. Jesus' love was so apparent that the crowd of mourners commented on it. Phileo *love is a deep friendship love that is evident to others. The recipients recognize that love as well.*

In Matthew 10:37 Christ proclaimed, "He who loves father or mother more than Me is not worthy of Me; and he who loves son or daughter more than Me is not worthy of Me." Jesus used the word *phileo* to describe the love people have for the members of their family, and yet Jesus called us to have an even greater *phileo* love for Him. Surely, if Christ desired us to love Him with this friendship type of love, it is not an insignificant kind of love. Phileo *love is the strong, often intense love we have for members of our family and close friends.*

In John 16:27 Jesus spoke with His disciples about boldness in prayer because "the Father Himself [*phileo*] loves you, because you have [*phileo*] loved Me and have believed that I came forth from the Father." If our heavenly Father loves us with such warmhearted affection, then *phileo* love must be a love worth having for our husbands. *Even our Father in heaven loves us with* phileo *love!*

Also compelling is the fact Paul pronounced a judgment in 1 Corinthians 16:22 on anyone who does not *phileo* love the Lord. *Phileo* love must be some kind of love if we are put under a curse for not properly showing it toward the Lord Jesus! *Jesus is worthy of our* phileo *love.*

Jesus Himself proclaimed He loves us with this kind of love in Revelation 3:19: "Those whom I love, I reprove and discipline; therefore be zealous and repent." Phileo *love does what is best for others and actively participates in doing good to them.*

After Peter's denial of Jesus, Jesus examined Peter's heart and motives by asking him three questions in John 21:15-17. Jesus asked him, "Do you [*agape*] love Me?" In other words, Do you love Me with a great, broad love? To which Peter replied, "Yes, Lord; You know that I [*phileo*] love You." I love You with a personal love and devotion. I love You dearly.

Jesus asked him again, "Do you [*agape*] love Me?" Do you love Me with compassion and kindness? To which Peter again replied, "Yes, Lord; You know that I [*phileo*] love You." I love You with great affection.

It was then that Jesus asked Peter, "Simon, son of John, do you [*phileo*] love Me?" Do you really esteem Me as a close friend above all others? Peter grew more grieved at this last heart-searching question, to which he humbly replied, "Lord, You know all things; You know that I [*phileo*] love You." Lord, You know my heart. You know how devoted I am to You. I love You.

What a comfort it was for Peter to appeal to Christ's omniscience in this matter. Earlier, Peter had denied Christ to save his own skin. And yet in spite of his rash behavior, he did love Christ, but feared to proclaim it boldly in the wake of his fainthearted denunciation of Jesus. Jesus knew the inner workings of Peter's heart and understood the bighearted fisherman's fervent devotion for his Savior.

Matthew Henry, commenting on Jesus' threefold request to Peter, stated, "He [Peter] had a high esteem and value for Him, a grateful sense of His kindness, and was entirely devoted to His honour and interest; his desire was towards Him, as one he was undone without; and his delight in Him, as one he should be unspeakably happy in."[1]

In writing about Peter's love for Christ, Matthew Henry helps us understand the kind of love we are to have for our husbands. Phileo *love delights in the other person and places the other person above all others in the thoughts, emotions, and actions.*

We find a similar definition in Ephesians 5:33 in the Amplified Bible:

> Let the wife see that she respects and reverences her husband—that she notices him, regards him, honors him, prefers him, venerates and esteems him; and that she defers to him, praises him, and loves and admires him exceedingly.

When we put love and respect into practice, they look exactly the same. *Phileo* love is seen in the things we do to show the great affection we have for our husbands. *Phileo* love is emotional and strong. God the Father and Christ both love us this way, and they desire that we love them with that same strong love and delight. Love like this puts wings to any duty and gives us the grace to persevere through even the most difficult of times. Is it any wonder God commands us to love our husbands with this kind of love?

Your Husband Is Your Priority

Titus 2:4 tells older women to make it a priority to teach younger women to fervently love their husbands. This training program is for every married woman no matter how long she has been married. And there's great value in remembering to make your husband a priority. Continued training so that you are always making progress is easier than retraining after failing to make your husband a priority and developing bad habits. That is why the older women are called upon to teach the younger women about loving their husbands.

Making Your Husband a Priority

Why would young women need help in this area? After all, aren't couples usually still starstruck with each other in the beginning of a marriage? Yet if you are newly married, it is quite possible you are also a new mother, which means your home is filled with children who need your love and attention too. Life can get hectic when you're fully occupied with diapers and ABCs, runny noses and potty training, sticky fingers and sweet kisses. Sometimes thinking about your husband is the last thing on your mind. Husbands can get shuffled to the side during this season of your life. You need to fight against neglecting your husband while you see to the needs of the little ones in your home. Older women can give wise counsel on how to do that. Your children will all grow up and leave home someday—if you are doing your job right— and you will one day find yourself sitting at home alone with that man you married years ago. Prepare for the future by working to make your marriage a priority. You children will benefit tremendously when you focus on loving your husband.

Eight Practical Ways to Make Your Husband a Priority

Think about him. Your heart always follows what your mind dwells on.

Do his stuff first. He will be blessed when he sees you putting his things at the top of your to-do list.

Maintain an identity as a couple even while you develop your identity as parents. This means spending time together. Even at home you can spend time together. If you establish a regular bedtime for your children, then you can have uninterrupted time together to talk and catch up on the day. You can even train your children when they are a little older not to interrupt "Mommy and Daddy's Talk Time." Make a commitment to have regular date nights. Trade babysitting duty with another couple or two, and get out and spend time together. Husbands thrive upon their wives' undistracted attention.

Look forward to his homecoming and teach the kids to look forward to it too. Prepare yourself, your kids, and your home for your husband's arrival. Brush your teeth, comb your hair, tidy up the house, have something cooking for dinner, and have everyone lined up for hugs at the front door.

Be at home when he is home. Many young wives wait until dad comes home to do their errands because it is easier on them. Instead, take care of your errands while dad is at work so you can spend time together as a family. (If you need help training your little darlings so you can go out in public without embarrassing the family, then be sure to read the next chapter.)

Pray for him. There is nothing like praying for someone to motivate us to put our love into action. Praying for your husband will help you to love him better.

Make your relationship with your husband a priority over the other friendships you have. Because we women tend to "connect" more easily with other women, it is easy to end up focusing on those relationships above the priority of loving our husbands. Make your husband your best earthly friend.

From the first year of your marriage to your sixty-first year, plan on and look forward to times of intimacy with your husband. Nothing communicates priority more to a man than his wife's eagerness and willingness to meet his needs in this way. *You* are the *only* person on earth who can do this for him.

Biblical loving is a thought-out kind of love. It thinks about
and seeks to do what is best for the other person.

How One Sinner Can Love Another Sinner

If you have been married for longer than a month you have probably discovered your husband is not always Prince Charming. As wonderful as your husband may be, he is still a sinner who cannot read your
mind, who may not "clue in" as quickly as you would like, and who
thinks like a man, of all things! These are among the reasons we need to
be trained to love our husbands in a biblical manner—from *eros* love to
phileo love to *agape* love! Biblical loving is a thought-out kind of love. It
thinks about and seeks to do what is best for the other person.

Notice the *agape* type of love described to us by the apostle Paul in
1 Corinthians 13:4-7:

> Love is patient, love is kind and is not jealous; love does not
> brag and is not arrogant, does not act unbecomingly; it does
> not seek its own, is not provoked, does not take into account
> a wrong suffered, does not rejoice in unrighteousness, but
> rejoices with the truth; bears all things, believes all things,
> hopes all things, endures all things.

Did you catch the fact that emotions, feelings, and intuitions are
not mentioned in the verses above—only actions? Love *acts* toward
others for their good. Consider how you can apply those love verses to
your marriage. What are some ways you can extend patience to your
husband or act more kindly to him? Are you exhibiting jealousy when
you need to demonstrate patience and generosity as you let him serve
other people? Do you pout or manipulate him? What are some ways
you can unselfishly serve your husband? Are you making times of intimacy with your husband a priority? How can you overcome feelings
of irritation so you can respond with warm affection toward him? Do
you forgive him as quickly and completely as the Lord Jesus has forgiven you? Do you lead your husband into sin, or do you help him to
stand firm and encourage him to do what is right?

You can encourage your husband's spiritual growth by helping him get some undistracted time with the Lord, or helping him go to bed at a reasonable hour so he can begin his day with the Lord. Loving your husband biblically is not always convenient or easy for you; in fact, it always requires sacrifice. But if it helps your husband grow in godliness, then the extra effort on your part is well worthwhile.

How to Keep the Home Fires Burning

We need to be trained to kindle romance in our marriages. If you have been married for a while, you may have noticed that romance when you are first dating and romance after marriage are two very different things. Romance when you are *dating* is tied to all the firsts—the *first time* he looked long and deep into your eyes, the *first time* he held your hand, the *first time* he kissed you, the *first time* he told you he loved you. Experiencing romance while dating is primarily about the adventure of getting to know someone.

Romance *in marriage* is different because you've already experienced all those first things together, so the goose bumps and tingles that come with all those first things are gone. Instead, romance in marriage is kindled by making your husband a priority and continually looking for ways to encourage, surprise, and minister to him. Romance in marriage comes from thinking of ways you can please your husband and then doing those things!

We find a great principle for maintaining marital romance in Revelation 2:4-5. Do you remember Jesus' haunting words to the church at Ephesus? "I have this against you, that *you have left your first love.*" How can we avoid forgetting our "first love," our husbands? Jesus said, "Remember from where you have fallen, and repent and *do the deeds you did at first.*" Jesus told the believers in Ephesus to remember the love they had for Him at the beginning. He then told them to repent. They needed to turn from their neglect of Him and to return to doing the deeds they had done at first.

Here then is the principle you can apply to your marriage: You must remember what it was like when you and your sweety were first dating or in the early days of your marriage. If things are not like they once were, you must repent of whatever it is that has caused you to neglect your love. And finally, you can begin again to do the kinds of things you did at first that produced so much romance in your relationship.

In what ways did you communicate your love and delight in being married to the man God had given you? Did you place love notes in his lunch box? Did you go with him to the hardware store *without complaining*? Did you argue over who got to serve the other person? Were you eager and available for times of intimacy? Did you laugh at his jokes? The question for you today is this: Are you still doing those things, or have you "left" your first love? Do you need to repent of allowing your marriage to settle into a humdrum routine? Keep the zing and tingle alive in your marriage by doing the deeds you did at first to communicate your love to your hubby.

How to Love Him His Way

Because biblical love is other-focused rather than self-focused, we must seek to love our spouse in the ways that make him feel loved. You may find it hard to believe, but some men would rather go fishing with their wives than go shopping! Loving your husband in a way that makes *him* feel loved can be a difficult task because it may not come naturally or easily to you. Generally when we choose to show love to other people, we often end up showing love in the ways that make *us* feel loved.

For example, generally a woman feels loved when her husband talks with her and shares his thoughts, feelings, and motivations with her. However, many men don't feel loved when their wives arrange a candlelight dinner to talk about *feelings*! They may appreciate the effort and enjoy the time with their wife, but why "waste" the ambiance of candlelight on simply *talking*? Though in-depth conversations may be the very thing that pegs the needle on your love scale, it may hardly register on his. And not only are men and women different from each other, but each person is different as well. The solution lies in thinking of what makes your *husband* feel loved, rather than trying to love him in the same ways that make *you* feel loved.

Women, you need to become a student of your mate. Study him!

Find out what makes him feel the most loved by you. Remember, most men feel loved when their wives ensure there are times of regular intimacy in their marriage. (Ladies, ask your husband what he considers "ideal" in this area and what is "just enough," and then endeavor to love him within this range.) Philippians 2:3-4 provides the mindset we need to maintain if we are going to excel in this area: "Do nothing from selfishness or empty conceit, but with humility of mind regard one another as more important than yourselves; do not merely look out for your own personal interests, but also for the interests of others." Find out what your husband's interests are and try to meet them.

What makes your husband feel loved? Ask him.

"Warm fuzzies" in marriage come when we pay attention to the details, so it is important we notice them! Are you sure the things you are doing to show your love to your spouse are things that make *him* feel loved, or are they things that make *you* feel love for him? Write down the things *you know* make your spouse feel loved and special. For instance, *I know* my husband loves surprises. Whether I give him a surprise or he plans one for me doesn't matter—he loves surprises. *I also know* my husband feels loved if I hover around him when he is working outside or when I go along for the ride to Home Depot. *What makes your husband feel loved? Ask him.*

Love Your Husband Intimately

While I was writing this chapter my husband asked me, "Did you include a section on sexual intimacy?" Later he asked me if I needed his help writing this section. I think he was afraid I would forget to tell you about this important aspect of marriage, so here it is! Ladies, *love your husband by meeting his sexual needs.* You're the only person in all the world who can do this for him. And God has given you this special privilege to joyfully obey. We learn some important principles about this area of marriage when we read Paul's instructions about ways to overcome sexual immorality in 1 Corinthians 7:3-5:

The husband must fulfill his duty to his wife, and likewise also the wife to her husband. The wife does not have authority over her own body, but the husband does; and likewise also the husband does not have authority over his own body, but the wife does. Stop depriving one another, except by agreement for a time, so that you may devote yourselves to prayer, and come together again so that Satan will not tempt you because of your lack of self-control.

God has ordained husbands and wives to meet each other's sexual needs. When you marry, your body is no longer your own, but belongs to your husband. You are not to deprive your husband of "access" to your body except for the purpose of prayer, and only if you both agree to it, and then you are to come together again so neither of you are tempted to engage in immorality.

One of the ways you can help your husband in the area of sexual temptation is to *regularly* meet his sexual needs. This will serve as a protection for him and for you. You may not feel vulnerable to immorality, but God says you are vulnerable. God says you need to come together to enjoy the physical and spiritual oneness of sexual intimacy or you will create a greater vulnerability to adultery. Find out about your husband's sexual needs, likes, and dislikes, and be sure to communicate to him about your own needs and preferences so he can fulfill his responsibility to you as well. Contentment and satisfaction with sexual intimacy is a strong indicator of the health of your marriage, so work at meeting each other's needs.

Making Your Marriage a Priority Never Ends

We can always excel still more at loving our husbands. There will never come a time when we don't need to make our marriages a priority. Almost yearly my husband teaches some type of marriage class at church or preaches a series of sermons on marriage, and every time he does, we find something we need to work on in our marriage because we continue to change and grow. All too easily we can become a little complacent or let our focus shift to other things. We find we need frequent reminders to make our marriage a priority. Even after being married more than 25 years there are still ways I can improve in loving my husband.

Paul tells us in Ephesians 5:27 that the marriage relationship is to represent to the world how Christ loves His bride, the church. We worship God by obeying Him, and one way we worship Him is by obeying His command to love our husbands. Isn't that amazing? By faithfully making your husband a priority, you bring God glory.

That's why you should diligently love your husband, and seek to honor and encourage him. In doing so you will bring honor to the Lord as others observe your faithfulness. And may those who observe you proclaim, "An excellent wife, who can find? For her worth is far above jewels. The heart of her husband trusts in her, and he will have no lack of gain. She does him good and not evil all the days of her life" (Proverbs 31:10-12).

1. The Greek word Paul uses for love in Titus 2:4 is *phileo*. The word *phileo* is generally summed up as the friendship kind of love, which is sometimes dismissed as not being a fervent or worthy kind of love to have. Yet that is not true. Look up the following verses and note who is being loved and the characteristics of that love: Matthew 10:37; John 11:3,36; 16:27; 21:15-17; 1 Corinthians 16:22; and Revelation 3:19.

2. Based on your observations from the verses above, write out a description of *phileo* love.

3. Why do young women need to be trained to *phileo* love their husbands?

4. *Phileo* love pays attention to the details. If you are married, write down the things you know make your spouse feel loved and special. You can practice loving others even if you are not married. Think of a friend or family member, and write down the things you can do for him or her to let that person know you care.

5. Now, are you *doing* the things you wrote in answer to the question above? When was the last time you did something special for your spouse? Are you sure the things you are doing to show your love to your husband are things that make *him* feel loved, or are they things that make *you* feel love for him?

6. A special project for you: Come up with a special way to show love toward your husband this week, then observe the resulting response. What does that teach you about your husband? If you aren't married, choose a family member or close friend you desire to bless and devise a *phileo* love project for him or her, then note the response. What insight does the response give you into the heart of your friend or family member?

Chapter 9

The Art of Loving Your Children

We've all encountered the frustrated and embarrassed parent who tries to maintain some semblance of decorum while dealing with their pint-sized misbehaving offspring. It happened to me again when I was preparing to purchase some items at Costco. An immaculately dressed woman got in the line next to mine. In her shopping cart was her son—sporting a scowl on his face about a mile wide. The boy looked at least six or seven years old, but he acted like he was four. I hope he was just tall for his age, because if he was as old as he looked, then she was in trouble already.

The boy's voice tones rose and fell petulantly as he whined about "something." His mother, who looked competent to oversee a multitude of emergencies, was reduced to playing *Let's Make a Deal* with her son. She coaxed and cajoled him, trying to head off a temper tantrum. She tried bribing him with ice cream and playtime at the park, both of which did not forestall the impending scene. Like a cloudburst, the boy's tantrum broke in all its terrible glory upon all of us who were standing in the lines nearby. The mother's face turned red as she tried to deal with her son, while continuing to wear a pasted-on smile. I was embarrassed for her and tried not to add to her shame by watching the ensuing drama, but it was hard not to stare as the boy sounded off like a police siren.

Every parent has had to deal with a child's meltdown in public at least once, and thankfully God's Word provides help for parents. It teaches us how to prevent child meltdowns and how to proceed when one occurs. Above all, the Bible provides the framework *every* parent, potential parent, and innocent bystander needs to know for raising children who love the Lord and desire to honor Him with their lives. From Titus 2:3-5 we can begin to build the foundation for the most biblical and God-pleasing way of loving our children even on melt-down days!

Trained to Love Our Children

The older women have their work cut out for them! Not only are they to train the younger women how to love their husbands, but they are also to aid the younger women in loving their children. God desires women to be *trained* to love their children. What an interesting thought! Why would we mothers need to be *trained*—of all things—to love our children? You might find yourself thinking, *Of course I love my children. I'm a woman—it's natural for women to love their children. That's what we do.* Yet God's Word tells us we need to learn how to love our children in the way that is best for them and that brings God glory.

The world teaches that mothering is "natural" and all we need to do is give birth to a baby and start doing what "feels right," but the Bible says something different. God says mothers and mothers-to-be need to be trained to love their children biblically. More often than not it means we need to learn to do things differently than what comes "naturally." Sometimes it means *unlearning* what came naturally to us. Instead of doing what *we* think is right, we are to do what *God* says is right and follow His plan when it comes to loving our children.

> How you raise or train up your children will—
> to a large degree—determine how much
> you delight in and enjoy your children.

Not only are women to be *trained* to love their children, they are to have *phileo* love for their children. In the previous chapter we learned women are to *phileo* love their husbands by making them a prior-ity, showing fervent love and devotion to them, and enjoying a deep friendship with them. In a similar manner, God desires women to delight in loving their children. God intends for parents to *enjoy* their children, and it is this quality that is at the heart of *phileo* love. The idea inherent to the command of Titus 2:4 is to train our children so wisely and so biblically that *even other people* like spending time with them!

The Scriptures attest that how you raise or train up your children will—to a large degree—determine how much you delight in and enjoy your children. If you apply diligence in teaching and training your children, which the Bible says is the same as loving them, then you will reap the blessing of having children you love and enjoy being with. I think of this whenever I hear moms say, "I can't wait for summer to end and for school to start again. My kids are driving me crazy." Some moms say such things in moments of exasperation, but others really mean it. They don't enjoy having their kids around and don't mind letting them know about it. What a shame for any mother to feel like that when God can teach us how to parent so we delight in our children.

Many parents think they are loving their children when they turn a blind eye and deaf ear to their rebellion. But is that really love? The Bible says love covers a multitude of sins, but God commands parents to raise children who are respectful and obedient, and who love God and honor their parents. If our children are not loved so as to lead them to Christ and make them blessings to others, then we are missing the whole point of parenting.

J.C. Ryle, a pastor in England during the late 1800s, wrote a powerful and practical little booklet called *The Duties of Parents*. This booklet is a must-read for every parent. He concludes his wise counsel with these words:

> Fathers and mothers, I charge you solemnly before God and the Lord Jesus Christ, take every pain to train your children in the way they should go. I charge you for the sake of your own future comfort and peace. Truly it is in your interest so to do. Truly your own happiness in great measure depends on it. Children have ever been the bow from which the sharpest arrows have pierced man's heart.[1]

Ryle is right! The love and joy we find in our children is linked to the way we train them. It is not that we withhold love from our children if they don't behave like we want them to—perish the thought! No, it is that children left to themselves will not learn to serve others or seek the Lord. This is why God desires we teach and train our children. They don't know the right way to go. It's up to us to teach them, and as we train them they grow ever more enjoyable to be around.

The Source of Parenting Wisdom

The Bible makes it clear the fear of the Lord is the beginning of wisdom, even when it comes to parenting. Psalm 111:10 reads, "The fear of the LORD is the beginning of wisdom; a good understanding have all those who do His commandments." Only by obeying God's Word will we do what is best for our children, bring glory to God, and have the greatest chance of experiencing peace and harmony in our home. We will *know* we are doing what is best if we follow God's guidebook for parents.

The key to raising likeable, wise children *begins* by clinging to God and His Word. Many enter parenthood with some sort of "philosophy" they intend to adhere to, others "wing it" and do what comes naturally, and some read parenting books written by those who have no desire to honor the Lord. Yet any school of thought we subscribe to must be filtered through God's Word. The Bible itself contains all the wisdom and instruction we need for raising kids who love Him and who we, and others, love to be around. Children are too precious to experiment on. We must *prepare* to parent, not wing it, by following the time-tested and proven principles in Scripture.

For example, some might say, "The Bible doesn't say there is anything wrong with children throwing temper tantrums." They might argue that it's okay to let your child scream and throw himself on the floor when he doesn't get his way. Now, while the Bible may not specifically use the term *temper tantrum* to describe that thing your toddler does when he is upset, it does have plenty to say about outbursts of anger, selfishness, and rebellion. It's our responsibility as parents to search God's Word for the commands and principles related to parenting and to use them to train our children. Then when our toddler has temper tantrums, we can confront, correct, instruct, and encourage him in the right way according to God's Word.

The Scope of Your Training

Titus 2:4 gives only the general instruction for women to love their children, but other texts in the Bible are specific about *how* we are to love them. One of the great parenting passages in the Bible is Deuteronomy 6:4-7, which contains the focus and scope of *what* you are to train your children. Even if you have never studied any other passage on parenting, these few verses contain everything you need to know about raising great kids who have a love and respect for the Lord. If you add the rest of what the Bible says about parenting to Deuteronomy 6:4-7, you will have a well-stocked toolbox that will help you raise obedient, respectful, hardworking children who love the Lord and the things of the Lord.

Know God Intimately

In Deuteronomy 6:4 we read, "The LORD is our God, the LORD is one." These truths about God form the foundation of our parenting. Actually, they form the foundation for our whole life. When we consider the statement, "The LORD is our God, the LORD is one," we realize we must first know who God is, and secondly, we must come to know Him personally—He must be *our* God. It's not enough to just know *about* God, we must know Him intimately. *How can you introduce your children to a God you don't know?*

The "Romans Road" explains how we can know God personally. In Romans 3:10 we read about our problem: "There is none righteous, not even one." Romans 3:23 explains why we have a problem: "All have sinned and fall short of the glory of God." Our sin separates us from God. Not only do we sin ourselves, but it is our inherited nature passed down to us from Adam. Sin entered the world in the Garden of Eden when Adam sinned, and was then passed down to us, as it says in Romans 5:12: "Therefore, just as through one man sin entered into the world, and death through sin, and so death spread to all men, because all sinned." Just like dogs give birth to dogs, so sinners give birth to sinners.

The consequence of engaging in even one sin is death, as Romans 6:23 states. But that verse also says, "The free gift of God is eternal life in Christ Jesus our Lord." We are deserving of death because of the sins we have committed against God, but God provided a way for us to live—and that is through sending Jesus Christ to die for our sins. As Romans 5:8 says, "God demonstrates His own love toward us, in that while we were yet sinners, Christ died for us."

Knowing that no one is righteous enough to please God, we must go to the One who was—the Lord Jesus Christ. Only Jesus lived a perfect and holy life on earth. And only He could serve as the perfect sacrifice able to take away our sins. If we come to Jesus Christ in faith, turning away from our old life of sin and desiring to live our lives for Him, then we will be saved, as Romans 10:9 says: "If you confess with your mouth Jesus as Lord, and believe in your heart that God raised Him from the dead, you will be saved." Verse 13 goes on to say, "Whoever will call on the name of the Lord will be saved."

> Our love for God authenticates what we
> say about Him to our children.

If we desire to instruct our children in the ways of the Lord, then we must know Him as our Lord and Savior, and seek to know Him and follow Him all the days of our lives.

Love God Completely

Deuteronomy 6:5 explains what seeking and following the Lord will look like in our lives. We are to love God with all our heart, all our soul, and all our might. Loving God is the next building block in our parenting foundation. First, we must know Him personally. And next, our relationship with the Lord is to be characterized by fervent love for Him. Our love for God authenticates what we say about Him to our children. Kids know when we truly believe in and love something. And our love for the Lord, observable by what we say and do, validates and proves what we teach our children about God.

Do you talk about the Lord? Do you enjoy reading His Word for yourself and to your children? Do you want to obey the Lord? When you sin, do you repent quickly and desire to become right with Him? Do you love the things that God loves—righteousness, His Word, other believers? *How can your children tell you love God?*

Hide His Word in Your Heart

The next layer in our parenting foundation, after knowing and loving the Lord, comes from Deuteronomy 6:6, where we learn the Word of God is to be in our heart. That's an easy concept to understand, but putting God's Word in our hearts takes more than good intentions. It means taking the time to read our Bible, think about the ways of God, memorize Scripture passages that help us to combat sin and strengthen our walk, and listen to sermons at church or even on an iPod. *Are you an example to your children of how to hide God's Word in your heart?*

Seek Him Diligently

Once we know and love God by hiding His Word in our hearts, we possess the single greatest resource for parenting. Deuteronomy 6:7 says we are then to take God's precious Word and *diligently* teach what we know. To teach with diligence speaks of the intensity with which we are to train our children in the Word. We are to teach our children about God with constant and earnest effort and application. This goes hand in hand with Titus 2. We are to work on the roles and responsibilities of Titus 2:3-5 faithfully, persistently, and with zeal. We can't love our children without diligently training them in the Word of God. *Are you faithfully teaching your children about the Lord?*

Teaching our children about the Lord begins with Bible stories and songs when they are babies, and grows from there. Reading to your children will allow you to talk with them about the Lord and answer their questions. Amazing conversations can happen during reading time.

Use Every Opportunity

So how can we begin teaching our children about the Lord? The Lord provided practical instruction on just how to do this—Deuteronomy 6:7 says we are to talk about God and His ways when we sit down, when we walk, when we lie down, and when we rise up. What a blessing this little portion of Scripture is for parents! *Every life situation is an opportunity to talk with your children about the Lord.* When you are in the garden you can teach your little ones about the care and detail God put into creation. When you are doing chores together you can talk to them about how God wants us to work and what kinds of attitudes are pleasing to Him. Driving places together presents boundless opportunities to share what you have learned during your quiet times. Take advantage of life situations to talk with your children about the Lord. Those conversations will give your kids insight into your own walk with the Lord.

> God wants us to depend on Him when
> it comes to raising our children.

Principles for Training Your Children

While the Bible provides us with some principles for parenting, an exact step-by-step formula is largely absent from Scripture. However, what the Bible does tell us about parenting is sufficient to raise any child in any situation. Parenting is not meant to be a "1-2-3-all done" kind of thing. God uses children to teach parents to rely on Him. As we encounter difficult situations in our parenting we are driven to seek the Lord in prayer and trust Him. God wants us to depend on Him when it comes to raising our children. He wants us to consider His Word and seek to apply it to our parenting.

Proactive Parenting

As we study, pray, and learn about parenting we become proactive in our approach to parenting rather than reactive. Proactive parents study the Scriptures and carefully think about how to apply them in their children's lives before they are born or get to the next stage of development. A proactive parent is prepared *before* situations arise. This prevents last-minute "experimenting" on God's precious gift of children. A proactive parent considers the following questions:

- Have you thought about what kind of children you want to raise?

- What does *the Bible* say about the kind of child God wants you to raise?

- Have you considered what kinds of character qualities you want to instill in your children?

- What does *the Bible* say about those qualities?

- What does *the Bible* say about the steps you need to take to train your child's character?

- What does *the Bible* say about when you should start implementing your parenting plan?

Thinking about those questions, and then acting upon them, will help you to become *proactive* as a parent. If you were going to buy a car, would you do some research first? Or if you were going on vacation, would you make travel plans first? Children are far more important than cars or vacations, yet often we spend more time planning to buy a car or go on a vacation than we do preparing to parent our children. Make sure you have a plan based on the Word of God.

Now if you don't like the idea of having a plan for parenting, and you just want things to happen on their own, then consider the dangers of such an approach. Don't deceive yourself. Whether you parent with a plan or parent through abdication your children are still being trained, and you are still responsible before God for your children. Because our children are born with a sin nature they are not "naturally" going to turn out "good." It takes effort, diligence, and the application of God's Word to turn little sinners into little blessings.

Practical Help from Proverbs

Once we understand that the foundation of our parenting is built upon knowing God and loving Him, then we can turn to Scripture for the practical tools that will help with our construction project. And the book of Proverbs is especially full of wisdom for every parent. The goal is to become adept at recognizing the principles we can apply to our families, and then craft ways to employ them. The few examples that follow are only a handful of the parenting guidelines you can find in Proverbs. Let's take a look!

Start Early

When should parents begin to lovingly train their children? As early as possible, according to Proverbs 19:18: "Discipline your son while there is hope, and do not desire his death." The phrase "while there is hope" tell us that we have a limited amount of time to capture our children's hearts and instill God's Word in them. We need to take advantage of opportunities to teach our children while they are still young.

Jack and I began training our children early. As soon as they started crawling and getting into things, we introduced them to commands such as "No" and "No touch." Of course, for a short time they didn't understand what those words meant, but like any kind of language acquisition, hearing those words spoken repeatedly in the same circumstances taught them the meaning. Then along with the "No touch" command we would then redirect baby to a safer play item or remove the item altogether.

Many parents proudly relate how their 12-month-old baby can say a dozen words, but for some reason those same parents don't think their little one can understand what the word *no* means. Children are smart, and quickly learn how to rebel and deceive. You don't even have to teach them how to do this. It comes naturally. Even at a young age kiddos are adept at disobeying their parents. It is up to you to train them to obey you, and as a result, obey the Lord.

Use Reproof

Another parenting principle is found in Proverbs 3:11-12, which says,

"My son, do not reject the discipline of the LORD or loathe His reproof, for whom the LORD loves He reproves, even as a father corrects the son in whom he delights." We learn from these verses that the Lord disciplines those He loves, just as every loving parent reproves and disciplines their children. Learning how to receive correction is an essential character trait no matter what our age. We do our children good when we teach them how to listen humbly to reproof and repent of any wrongdoing.

Wise parents teach their children the very things they will need to know in order to follow the Lord for themselves. Think about it like this: How does God want you to receive reproof? Does He want you to give excuses for your disobedience? Is it pleasing to the Lord if you harden your heart and grow angry when He disciplines you? The Lord desires you to receive His discipline humbly, with sorrow over sin and a teachable spirit. Your goal is to train your children how to receive correction with that same kind of attitude, which paves the way for their willing obedience to the Lord too!

Remember, when children obey their parents they are obeying the Lord as well. Ephesians 6:1 says, "Children, obey your parents in the Lord, for this is right." When you train your children to obey you, ultimately you frame their hearts to obey the Lord. It doesn't guarantee your children's salvation, but it does train them to listen to instruction, receive it humbly, and learn from it.

Use Correction

Another principle for parenting appears in Proverbs 13:24: "He who withholds his rod hates his son, but he who loves him disciplines him diligently." God lovingly disciplines and trains every one of His children. And as parents, we are to follow His pattern as we train our own children. Parents who abdicate their responsibility in this area often say, "I love my children too much to spank them." What they are really saying is, "I love myself too much to do what God says is best for my children." The wise parent says, "I love my children too much not to spank them." Biblical discipline includes the whole range of the discipline process—encouragement, exhortation, correction, admonition, and chastisement.

The world disdains God's perfect plan for parenting and often rejects the idea of corporal punishment as an effective means of training our children. Yet God, our infinitely wise and loving Father, would never command us to do anything that would harm our children. There are some who abuse and misuse this means of training their children, but that doesn't negate the wisdom of *correctly* using corporal discipline.

Biblical discipline is self-controlled discipline. It is essential that every parent understand this truth. We must never enforce any kind of discipline when we are feeling angry or vengeful. Even yelling at our children is wrong. We must discipline in the fruit of the Spirit, which is "love, joy, peace, patience, kindness, goodness, faithfulness, gentleness, self-control" (Galatians 5:22-23). The goal of our discipline is to teach our children right from wrong, to instill in them a love for righteousness and a hatred for sin. But that can never be accomplished if we aren't parenting in the fruit of the Spirit.

It is impossible to obey God and train your children properly if you aren't under control yourself. That is sin. If you train your children to obey you the first time you give a direction, you can, to a great degree, train your children with a patient and gentle spirit. Often parents get in the habit of repeating commands to their children and end up threatening them with some punishment ("Susie, come to Mommy. *Susie*, Mommy said *come*. SUSIE! Don't make me count to three!"). Those kinds of interactions are exasperating to you and to your children. Train your children to obey you the first time, and if they willingly disobey, then *you must follow through* on your training by dealing out appropriate consequences in the fruit of the Spirit. If you need time to "get your act together" and recover a calm spirit, you can send your child to another room before giving out punishment. This also allows you to protect the dignity of the child by training him or her in private.

More Places to Find Help

We have barely scratched the surface of the parenting principles that are found in the book of Proverbs. This collection of wise sayings also provides counsel for parents in the areas of purity, work ethics, careful speech, self-control, overcoming conflict, and more. It is a parent's resource manual for child rearing. Take time to read through the book of Proverbs on a regular basis. Look for character qualities you desire to instill in your children, and consider how you can impart them. But remember that you need to apply in your own heart and life everything you are teaching your children!

> Parenthood is a privilege, and God has entrusted
> that precious treasure into your care.

You will also want to seek out older women who have raised children and whose lives reflect the godly qualities you want to instill in your own children. Ask those older women what they did to train their children during the different stages of childhood. There is a reason their kids turned out the way they did! Ask them how they applied God's Word in their parenting.

The Privilege of Training Your Children

How your children turn out depends a lot on you. God has given you His Word. He has given you resources in books, sermons, and spiritual mentors, but the training of your children is still *your* job. You must work against the attitude that says disciplining your children is a chore or an inconvenience. Nor should you ever think your kids are trying to make your life miserable. Parenthood is a privilege, and God has entrusted that precious treasure into your care.

I've seen mothers who respond to their children with an attitude that communicates, "You are such a nuisance. I can't believe I have to talk to you about this again." They clench their teeth, roll their eyes, and act like the teaching and training part of parenting was designed by God to be an inconvenience. *Your children need training—which is why they need you.* When you train your children, you are loving them in true Titus 2:4 fashion!

Every situation that involves training and discipline is an opportunity to prepare your children's hearts and minds in the ways of the Lord. Usually when mothers feel inconvenienced or become impatient, it is because they feel the training of their children is interrupting something "more important." Unfortunately, the things that usually seem so important at the time are rarely things that have eternal value. Usually we get caught up in our own agenda and find the "interruptions" from our children annoying. We are blind to the fact that we are being selfish. That's why it's necessary to think long-term, think eternally, get off the phone or the computer, put down the book, turn off the television, and take the time to lovingly train our children in a biblical and God-honoring way. The time we willingly invest in the raising up of our children will eventually bear fruit that brings joy to our hearts.

Hebrews 12:11 is a great help for the times when you grow weary of training your children. It states, "All discipline for the moment seems not to be joyful, but sorrowful; yet to those who have been trained by it, afterwards it yields the peaceful fruit of righteousness." If we keep our eyes on our parenting goal—to raise children who know and love the Lord and exhibit godly character, we will make those choices to turn the television off or put the book down, get out of our chair, and begin to deal with the hearts of our children. Every mother faces times when she is tempted *not* to discipline her children. But don't give up. If you are faithful to teach and train your children, you will see that peaceful fruit of righteousness begin to emerge in your children's lives.

God's ways are always best. And His magnificent wisdom in child-rearing has been recorded for us in the Bible. "Correct your son, and he will give you comfort; he will also delight your soul" (Proverbs 29:17) brings us back to where we started. No parent intends to raise foolish or rebellious children, but if we are not careful to apply God's wisdom, our children can end up bringing great sorrow to our souls. This is why Paul encourages the older women to teach the younger women how to biblically love their children. When we apply God's parenting principles within our families, we experience the joy and harmony God intended every family to experience. We will delight in our children and they, in turn, will bring joy to our hearts because they love the Lord and want to obey Him.

Oh, let us *love* our children with every ounce of our being, for this brings glory to the Lord!

1. How does correction in the life of a child contribute to family affection or *phileo* love? See Proverbs 10:1; 17:25; and 23:24.

2. What reasons does the Bible give for the need for correction? See Proverbs 3:12; 13:24; 22:15; and 29:15,17.

3. In what areas should you train your child? See Deuteronomy 4:9; 11:18-19; Psalm 78:5-8; Proverbs 2:1-5; and Ephesians 6:1-4.

4. One of the greatest compliments you can receive as a parent is when other people say they like spending time with your children. Do grandparents tremble at the idea of you bringing your little darlings over, or do Sunday school teachers smile wanly and rub a trembling hand over their foreheads when you come to pick up your child? These warning signs may indicate that you need to "love" your child in a more biblical manner as outlined in the verses above. How are you doing in this area?

5. Someone once said, "Train your child as though you won't have him next year. Treat your child as though he won't have you next year." What things would you focus on or quit doing if you had the time pressure of only one year?

6. Do you love your children enough to train them in godly character so others enjoy being around them? Choose one area to work on in your parenting and begin to implement it this week.

The Art of
Living Sensibly

For most women, when it comes to women's shoes, there are *cute* shoes, and then there are those other ones—the *sensible* ones. You know the ones I mean. We know we should buy the practical shoes—our feet would thank us, but oh, *the other kind*, the darling little shoes draw our eyes and wear down our more pragmatic considerations. They seem to whisper, "Remember, the right shoes can make the outfit." "Your feet won't hurt that much." "Look at how clunky those other shoes are. You don't need to wear *them*." If trying to decide which type of shoes to buy is a microcosm of our lives, then being *sensible* is not something we want to be.

For most of us, if we are given praise that includes the word *sensible*, we consider it a dubious compliment at best. Comments like "You are so sensible!" don't usually thrill us. More often the term inspires in us a feeling of dread—after all, sensible women wear sensible shoes and buy sensible purses and become the Christian equivalent of Spock on *Star Trek*—logical, fact-driven, and unfashionable in every facet of life. There is the idea that being sensible is somehow synonymous with being boring. With that in mind, it is particularly important that we dispel any misunderstandings or myths about what the word *sensible* means, for it is the next priority God wants us to apply in our lives.

What Does It Mean to Be Sensible?

In Titus 2:5, the New American Standard Bible translated the Greek word *sophrone* as "sensible." The King James Version used the word "discreet," while the New International Version and the English Standard Version both chose the word "self-controlled." Other less well-known Bible translations have used the word "sober." The English words *sensible, discreet,* and *self-controlled* appear to have little in common, so it seems odd that the Bible translators would use such dissimilar English words to translate the same Greek word. Yet it is the wide scope of words used in the different translations that shows us the breadth of the meaning of the Greek word used by Paul in Titus 2:5. This is why it is essential we comprehend its meaning. *If we don't understand the word correctly, we can grossly underestimate it and miss the opportunity to apply it to our lives.*

Let's take a moment to consider the meanings of the words used in the different Bible translations for the one Greek word in Titus 2:5. By reviewing each word's definition we'll gain more insight into this important priority. To be *sensible* means to have good sense or reason, while having *self-control* means to exercise restraint over one's own impulses or emotions. To be *discreet* means to show good judgment in conduct and speech, and possess the ability to discern the proper way to respond. *Prudent* is a synonym of discreet; it refers to being marked by wisdom and careful thought. And *sober* means to be serious, restrained, and moderate.

It is safe to say God prizes this quality of *sophrone* in His children. Paul used the same Greek word five times in his short letter to Titus (1:8; 2:2,5,6,12). It's obvious Paul knew the people on the island of Crete were lacking in sensibility, just as the Holy Spirit knew that believers in the future, like us, would need encouragement for sensible living as well.

Think about those new converts to Christianity on Crete, where Titus had been appointed to pastor. By their own admission they were "always liars, evil beasts, lazy gluttons" (1:12). People like this have no sense of self-control, no sense of moderation. In fact, they exercise *no sense* in many of life's decisions. They need others to teach them self-control, discretion, sober-mindedness—that is, how to be *sensible.* We could pity the Cretans' lack of sensibility, but the necessity for sensible living is as needful today as it was then. We need to learn about this priority too!

Women Still Need to Be Sensible

People's hearts haven't changed since the fall of Adam and Eve in the Garden of Eden. Eve, Sarah, Rahab, Ruth, and even the ladies on the island of Crete all needed to learn to be sensible. Women today are no different. *God knows what we need, and we need training in how to be sensible, discreet, prudent, and self-controlled.*

Every area of our lives benefits when we respond with discretion and self-control. Our relationships benefit when we respond sensibly and wisely, rather than relying on our feelings or responding rashly. Our parenting changes when we parent with self-control. It is not an accident that Titus 2:5 tells us to be "sensible" right after Titus 2:4 admonishes us to love our children. These two commands go hand in hand. Self-control, careful thought, and wise living are to character-ize our parenting. The same can be said for our relationship with our husbands. Every marriage needs restraint, wisdom, and self-control. The wisdom of God is evident when we consider this command to be sensible.

Even our relationship with Christ benefits when we live sensibly because what we think determines how we act and how we obey. We don't naturally possess God's wisdom and the ability to live it out, but when we become Christians and the Holy Spirit resides in us, we gain the mind of Christ and begin to think in new ways about everything. As we soak in the Scriptures, the Holy Spirit helps us take baby steps toward self-control, wisdom, and sensible living.

What Living Sensibly Looks Like

Being sensible is a quality dearly loved by God, and a quality He desires to see formed in us from the time of our salvation. Titus 2:11-12 highlights this truth: "The grace of God has appeared, bringing salva-tion to all men, instructing us to deny ungodliness and worldly desires and to live sensibly, righteously and godly in the present age." Ungod-liness and worldly desires are antithetical to sensible, righteous, and godly living—and it is to this way of life that God has called us.

When it comes to being sensible, God has not left us in the dark. The book of Proverbs has much to say about living in a sensible manner—in fact, Solomon explains his purpose in writing proverbs is to "give prudence to the naive, to the youth knowledge and discretion" (Proverbs 1:4). Because the Holy Spirit spoke through Solomon, by all means we should learn what He desires to teach us about being sensible. The book of Proverbs teaches us:

> "I, wisdom, dwell with prudence, and I find knowledge and discretion" (Proverbs 8:12). We learn that whenever and wherever you find God's wisdom, you will also find sensibility and prudence, which means a wise woman is also a sensible woman.

> "A fool's anger is known at once, but a prudent man conceals dishonor" (Proverbs 12:16). "A prudent man conceals knowledge, but the heart of fools proclaims folly" (Proverbs 12:23). A prudent and sensible woman has control over her emotions and doesn't speak rashly, even when she is sinned against.

> "Every prudent man acts with knowledge, but a fool displays folly" (Proverbs 13:16). A prudent woman considers and weighs her options before acting.

> "The wisdom of the sensible is to understand his way, but the foolishness of fools is deceit" (Proverbs 14:8). There is great wisdom in examining your weaknesses and the sins of the heart because doing so helps you move past those sins and toward the Lord and His ways. In fact, the wise woman can, by looking at her actions and daily choices, gain insight into her own heart.

> "A fool rejects his father's discipline, but he who regards reproof is sensible" (Proverbs 15:5). It is the sensible woman who listens to and heeds reproof, while a foolish woman rejects correction. Something as simple as how we respond to correction is a litmus test of our heart—wise or foolish, sensible or unteachable. The sensible woman considers her words and wisely knows when to keep silent for "even a fool, when he keeps silent, is considered wise; when he closes his lips, he is considered prudent" (Proverbs 17:28).

"The mind of the prudent acquires knowledge, and the ear of the wise seeks knowledge" (Proverbs 18:15). The woman of sense and discretion seeks wisdom from the Lord. She is not content with her own "wisdom," but desires to grow in the Lord's ways.

"The prudent sees the evil and hides himself, but the naive go on, and are punished for it" (Proverbs 22:3). The wise woman is careful in her proceedings and considers any dangers she may encounter, while a foolish woman rushes in and experiences the consequences of her rash behavior.

The book of Proverbs is a great place to learn what being sensible looks like as it is lived out each day. We also see that being sensible, prudent, discreet, and self-controlled are qualities that come from the Lord. A woman who desires to have these qualities in her life will ask the Lord for help in prayer, and will avail herself of wisdom as found in His Word. A woman who does this learns to exercise self-control over her emotions so she doesn't blurt out everything she is thinking or feeling. Instead, she learns to practice discretion in her speech. She gains wisdom and insight into her heart, and knows she can be deceived herself. She learns to consider her ways according to God's Word, rather than being led by her emotions.

God delights in the sensible woman.

The sensible woman learns to think—a lot! She thinks about the patterns she sees in her life and the motivations that drive her. She considers her ways and seeks to line them up with God's Word. And most important of all, she wisely listens to reproof. She listens to and heeds the corrective words that may come from reading God's Word, hearing the Word preached and taught, or may even come from the lips of a caring friend. All of which will help her grow in godliness. God delights in the sensible woman.

Growing More Sensible

Being sensible, self-controlled, prudent, and discreet are admirable qualities for every Christian. In the book of Titus, Paul commanded elders to be sensible, along with older men, women, and young men. Wise living is one of the effects of salvation upon our lives (Titus 2:12). So it is clear we must grow in this area—but how? How can we grow more sensible—more biblically sensible—and give glory to God in the process?

Proverbs 11:22 states, "As a ring of gold in a swine's snout so is a beautiful woman who lacks discretion." Ugh! Those words paint quite a picture, which is exactly what God intended when He moved Solomon to pen them. For a woman to lack discretion or restraint is akin to being a gold ring stuck into the nose of a disgustingly grimy pig. To avoid being a "ring of gold in a swine's snout" we must focus our attention on how we can grow in discretion, prudence, sense, and self-control. Below are eight practical ways every woman can grow in being sensible.

First, Turn Away from Sin

Being sensible begins with turning away from sin. First Corinthians 15:34 states, "Become sober-minded as you ought, and stop sinning; for some have no knowledge of God. I speak this to your shame." This command follows the wise admonition that "bad company corrupts good morals." No Christian will ever grow more like Christ, or more sensible, if he or she continues to engage in worldly pursuits. And even though you might not spend time with *people* who are bad company, it's possible for you to invite bad company into your home through the computer, television, and what you read.

Second, Recognize the Source of Wisdom

James 3:13 asks the question, "Who among you is wise and under-standing?" James then answers that we can tell whether someone is wise by looking at her life because wisdom shows up in her actions, her good behavior, and her right attitudes. When we act ungodly we don't exhibit godly wisdom, but rather man's wisdom, which is earthly, nat-ural, and demonic (James 3:14-15). James explains if we want to be wise and understanding then we must recognize *where* wisdom comes from: "The wisdom from above is first pure, then peaceable, gentle, reasonable, full of mercy and good fruits, unwavering, without hypocrisy" (verse 17). Godly wisdom comes from above, from God, and He forms wise, sensible character in those who seek Him. We seek godly wisdom when we read the Bible, listen to good sermons, memorize Scripture, and obey the Lord. As we pursue godly wisdom, God builds sensible and wise character in us.

Third, Fix Your Eyes on Heaven

A key component of becoming sensible and wise is to focus your eyes on heaven. First Peter 1:13 says, "Prepare your minds for action, keep sober in spirit, fix your hope completely on the grace to be brought to you at the revelation of Jesus Christ." When we remember the great debt of love we owe Christ for saving and redeeming us from sin and death, we are moved to eagerly fix our eyes on heaven and look forward to the day when we will see our Lord and Savior, Jesus Christ.

Fourth, Search the Scriptures

I once wanted to make a certain kind of Indian dish with a special kind of curry. I had to search for it in quite a few grocery stores before I found it. Without this special kind of curry I couldn't prepare the dish. In a similar way sensible living comes from searching the storehouse of God's Word for the ingredients we need to grow more sensible. Psalm 19:7-14 beautifully explains the benefits that come from making God's Word your source of wisdom. The Word of God is described as "perfect," "sure," "right," "pure," "clean," "true," "more desirable than gold," and "sweeter...than honey." That perfect Word then restores our soul, makes us wise, causes our hearts to rejoice, enlightens us, warns us, and helps us discern errors and sin. As we search and study God's Word, change will take place!

Fifth, Ask the Lord to Help You Grow in This Area

Pray! Keep praying! Ask God to help you grow more sensible. Paul beseeched the Lord on behalf of believers at Philippi that they would grow more discerning—more *sensible*. He wrote, "This I pray, that your love may abound still more and more in real knowledge and all discernment" (Philippians 1:9). Anytime we are lacking in any godly discipline it is wise to ask the Lord to help us grow in that area. If you realize you are struggling with discernment or being sensible, ask the Lord to help you. Share your requests with others so they can pray for you as well.

Sixth, Begin Applying What You Know

There always comes a point in our reading of Scripture that we are exhorted to put into practice what we know, and 2 Peter 1:5-7 is one such example. In this passage we are urged by Peter to *supply diligence* to our faith *by applying* moral excellence, knowledge, self-control, perseverance, godliness, brotherly kindness, and love. We are urged to grow in our faith through self-control, among other things. Am I a cook if I don't cook anything? Am I a housewife if I don't ever make an effort to keep house? No. You must turn your knowledge into *application*. The same is true when it comes to being sensible, self-controlled, and discreet. You must strive to *do* as well as know.

Seventh, Don't Let Your Age Be an Impediment

As we approach fifty years of age, my husband and I have noticed the effects of growing older are more pronounced. While growing older is a reality for all of us, we mustn't let it become an excuse for not pursuing a sensible life. On the other hand, Paul urges the young to live as an example: "Let no one look down on your youthfulness, but rather in speech, conduct, love, faith and purity, show yourself an example of those who believe" (1 Timothy 4:12). We can serve as an example at any age if we press on in godliness and seek the Lord as we become more sensible, prudent, and self-controlled.

> Self-control is built into our hearts and lives not by sheer
> grit-it-out willpower, but by relying upon the Lord to help us
> when we are tempted to give in to our lusts or emotions.

Eighth, Let Time Do Its Work

All character qualities take time to grow, and that's especially true about learning to be sensible. *It takes time* to overcome bad habits and reform them with God's Word. *It takes time* to build the foundation of God's Word in your heart so you can respond with godly wisdom when life gets sticky. *It takes time* to learn the art of discretion—when to speak up, and when to be quiet. Self-control is built into our hearts and lives not by sheer grit-it-out willpower, but by relying upon the Lord to help us when we are tempted to give in to our lusts or emotions. A sensible life is exemplified by a woman who seeks the Lord in prayer and through the Word of God, who leans upon Him throughout the day, and who desires above all else to have her responses be the kind that please the Lord.

There is an old hymn called "Take Time to Be Holy" which explains the process of growing more sensible day after day. As you read the hymn, see if you can identify some of the steps necessary for becoming sensible:

> Take time to be holy; speak oft with thy Lord;
> Abide in Him always, and feed on His Word.
> Make friends with God's children; help those who are weak,
> Forgetting in nothing His blessing to seek.
>
> Take time to be holy; the world rushes on;
> Spend much time in secret with Jesus alone.
> By looking to Jesus, like Him thou shalt be;
> Thy friends in thy conduct His likeness shall see.
>
> Take time to be holy; let Him be thy Guide;
> And run not before Him, whatever betide.
> In joy or in sorrow, still follow the Lord
> And, looking to Jesus, still trust in His Word.
>
> Take time to be holy; be calm in thy soul;
> Each thought and each motive beneath His control.
> Thus led by His Spirit, to fountains of love,
> Thou soon shalt be fitted for service above.[1]

Did you notice some of the steps you can take toward growing more sensible? Take time to be with the Lord in prayer and in the

Word. Spend time fellowshipping with and serving other believers. Seek the Lord's blessing by doing everything for Him and His glory. Don't neglect your private time with the Lord, for from this comes wisdom and discretion. Wait upon the Lord and trust Him, keeping your heart quiet in Him. When we submit ourselves to the Lord throughout the day, we grow in wisdom and sense—not common sense, not horse sense, but biblical sense.

By now we have gained a greater understanding of what it means to be sensible. And now all that's left is for us to take the steps necessary to live sensibly. Everyone has room to grow in this area, and the questions below can help each one of us assess ways we can grow more sensible.

- At what points in your life do you need to use careful, biblical reasoning?

- In what areas of your life do you need to exercise more self-control over your emotions, desires, and will?

- What are some ways you can exercise prudence and discretion in your conversations?

- What areas of your life do you feel are not characterized by sensible thought and conduct?

- What are some ways you can show godly judgment in your conduct and speech?

God is not calling us to drudgery or geekdom when He bids us to be sensible. In fact, God intends to bless us, which is why He made this character quality a priority. And the result of applying God's wisdom is that we bear much spiritual fruit—we will respond with discretion and self-control. Are you ready? Sensibility awaits!

Now, about those shoes…

The Art of Living Sensibly
Chapter 10 Study Questions

1. The next quality we see for women is that they are to be *sensible* (NASB), *discreet* (KJV), *self-controlled* (NIV). In English, these words don't seem like close synonyms at all. That variety in translation helps show the breadth of the Greek word (*sophrone*) used in Titus 2:5. It encompasses a wide area of meaning and it is important that we gain an understanding of it. Define each of the following words: *sensible, self-controlled, discreet, sober, temperate, prudent.*

2. The book of Proverbs has much to say about living in a sensible manner. What do you learn about those who are discreet, or prudent, or sensible? See Proverbs 1:1,4; 8:12; 12:16,23; 13:16; 14:8,15,18; 15:5; 17:28; 18:15; 19:14; and 22:3.

3. God prizes a sensible spirit in His children (men and women alike). How are you growing in this area? Do you prize this quality as much as God does? How can you develop an even greater love for being sensible?

4. From Titus 2:3-4 we learned that the older women are to train the young women to be sensible. In what ways might that training be accomplished? See Psalm 119:66; Philippians 1:9; 1 Timothy 4:12; and 1 Peter 1:22.

5. What are the different areas in which women need to learn to be sensible? (Don't forget the varied meaning of this word.)

6. Can you think of a time when someone helped you to be sensible (self-controlled, discreet, sober, temperate, or prudent)? How did that person help you? What was the result in your life?

7. Someone may say, "Being sensible sounds so boring! All that calm, rational thinking leaves no room for fun!" Write a response in defense of being sensible.

Chapter 11

The Art of
Pursuing Purity

I t's been a hot day working outside in the yard, and you are parched. There on the kitchen counter is a tall, ice-cold glass of sparkling clean water, ready for you to enjoy. You anticipate its freshness, but as you get ready to take a sip a gnat does a kamikaze into the glass. "Ewwwww!" you exclaim, and immediately you head to the sink to pour out the water.

Your son, who saw it all, helpfully suggests, "Mom, it's only a little gnat. It won't hurt you. Just take the gnat out and drink the water anyway." He smiles slyly and adds, "You know how you're always telling me to conserve water."

"Yuck!" you protest. "I can't drink that. It's not clean anymore. It has gnat cooties in it." At which point you dump the gnat-contaminated water into the sink and pour yourself a new, clean glass of water, quickly consuming it before your son has any more bright ideas.

Purity is an interesting concept, isn't it? One little tiny gnat is nothing compared to a large glass of water. Can one itty-bitty gnat really contaminate a whole glass of water? Before we answer, we need to keep in mind that purity is an absolute quality. For something to be pure, it has to be 100 percent pure, or it's defiled. Even if your water is 99.576 percent pure, the other .424 percent with a little bit of gnat mixed in is defiled. And who wants to drink that?

Purity Defined

And that brings us to the next priority from God according to the list in Titus 2:3-5: purity. In the same way that we want our water to be pure and free from insects with a death-wish, God desires us to be pure and free from sin and its defilements. Most Bible commentators believe the call to purity in Titus 2:5 is directed at chastity, modesty, and freedom from sexual immorality—of every kind and degree—because it rests between commands pertaining to the marriage relationship. So rather than concentrate on purity in terms of holy living (which we covered in detail in chapter 4, "The Art of Growing in Holiness"), we will focus our attention in this chapter on how we can remain physically pure (not engaging in sexual sin) *and* morally pure (in our thoughts and desires).

Attaining purity is a challenge because it takes only one "gnat" to introduce impurity or immorality into our lives. If you live where you have access to a television, a computer, magazines, billboards, iPods, or other people, then you know that the world's focus is antithetical to purity. And it's for this reason that God desires us to make our physical and moral purity a priority, regardless of our age, our season in life, or our relationship status. The way in which we implement purity in our lives reveals the *distinctive* characteristics of a believer.

Even then many women don't see the need to focus on their own purity. They may acknowledge there are times when the battle for purity is more pronounced and there are times when it's barely a blip on the radar screen. They believe purity—especially sexual purity of the body, mind, and heart—is something men struggle with, and that it's not such a big deal for women. But apparently God doesn't think like that. *For God included purity in His list of priorities in Titus 2:3-5.* So let's learn together, shall we? That will make it possible for each one of us to serve as a living, breathing example of purity in body, mind, and spirit.

Purity Is Essential

Purity is essential for *every* believer for a number of reasons. First, according to Titus 2:5, purity is a matter of love and obedience to the Lord because we are *commanded* to be pure. Jesus connected the dots between love and obedience when He taught on this topic in John

14:15: "If you love Me, you will keep My commandments." So we show our love for the Lord as we obey His command to be pure.

Second, our love and allegiance to the Lord is the *only* thing we are to be mastered by, so if our passions and desires have us in their grip, then we must escape. Psalm 119:133 reflects the desire of believers to be right before the Lord and overcome sin: "Establish my footsteps in Your word, and do not let any iniquity have dominion over me."

Another reason for purity is because *the Lord sees* everything we do—and think! Imagine if each time you had an impure thought it was flashed upon a huge movie screen for all to see. You probably shudder at the idea (I do!), but that is essentially what happens every time you engage in any kind of immorality—physical or mental. The Lord sees it all. There is nothing hidden from His sight (Hebrews 4:13).

Fourth, we want pure lives and hearts because of our *relationship* with the Lord. Matthew 5:8 says, "Blessed are the pure in heart, for they shall see God." Purity of heart—and mind and body—is a hallmark of believers, for they are the ones who shall see God. Because God has given us His Holy Spirit, we *desire* to walk in purity before Him, even though we often battle against our own lustful desires.

Not only is purity a characteristic of the new heart given at salvation, but *purity is also our purpose* according to 1 Thessalonians 4:7-8: "God has not called us for the purpose of impurity, but in sanctification. So, he who rejects this is not rejecting man but the God who gives His Holy Spirit to you." God has called and saved us to be holy and set apart—sanctified for good use, which requires that we remain pure.

> Every river has a source or place of beginning. And the Bible explains that our hearts are the starting point for purity.

Ultimately, we are called to have a pure heart, mind, and body because we are children of the Lord. We are to act like we belong to His family. First Peter 1:14-16 reminds us, "As obedient children, do not be conformed to the former lusts which were yours in your ignorance, but like the Holy One who called you, be holy yourselves also in all your behavior; because it is written, 'You shall be holy, for I am holy.'" Purity reveals our family connections!

Purity Begins in Our Hearts

Every river has a source or place of beginning. And the Bible explains that our hearts are the starting point for purity. While this sounds great, we do have a problem: Even though we have been born again and have received a new nature, we are still sinners. The good news is the transforming power of Christ is at work in us, yet we need to understand that sin still resides in us.

Listen to what Jesus had to say about the sins that lurk in the dark corners of our hearts: "From within, out of the heart of men, proceed the evil thoughts, fornications, thefts, murders, adulteries, deeds of coveting and wickedness, as well as deceit, sensuality, envy, slander, pride and foolishness. All these evil things proceed from within and defile the man" (Mark 7:21-23). Impure thoughts often lead to impure deeds. Nothing new there; we've learned that before. But what we didn't learn before is that when it comes to sexual impurity other people are often involved, which makes the need for purity even more important. Fornication, adultery, lesbianism, pornography, even immodesty are *external manifestations* of what we have been thinking. Isn't it shocking to discover the far-reaching effects our thoughts can have? I think so! It makes me want to guard my thoughts more diligently.

Proverbs 4:23 explains how we do this: "Watch over your heart with all diligence, for from it flow the springs of life." Solomon describes our heart as the springs of life because whatever dwells within our hearts will eventually show up in our lives. If we allow the crude oil of wicked thoughts and immorality to reside in our hearts, then sooner or later the black tar of those thoughts will float to the surface of our heart and take shape in wicked deeds. Paul explains in Titus 1:15, "To the pure, all things are pure; but to those who are defiled and unbelieving, nothing is pure, but both their mind and their conscience are defiled." Once the spring is defiled, everything in the river that flows from it is defiled. That's why we must guard our hearts "with all diligence" if we are to remain pure.

Purity Is Revealed in Our Conduct

When we cleanse our hearts daily through confession and repentance and wash ourselves with the pure water of God's Word, our conduct will be pure too. Second Timothy 2:22 states, "Now flee from youthful lusts and pursue righteousness, faith, love and peace, with those who call on the Lord from a pure heart." A pure life demands that we flee from our ungodly desires and temptations and seek after the things God loves. To do that, we must turn our eyes away from things that may tempt us.

If we find ourselves listening to music that places tempting thoughts in our minds, we must replace our choice of music with something that will help us "call on the Lord from a pure heart." Sometimes the grocery store plays disco music from the 1970s that I find tempting. (Try not to laugh!) That music takes me back to the days when I used the dance floor to attract attention to my body in hopes some guy would ask me out. So when I hear those familiar tunes, my mind easily reverts to those old ways of thinking. What that means for me is that *even now*, light years away from that time in my youth, I must keep my guard up whenever I am in the cereal aisle and hear the Bee Gees cue up!

Second Timothy 2:22 also tells us that fleeing youthful lusts is made more effective by spending time with other believers who encourage us to pursue purity. It's important to remember that those who want to indulge their flesh usually isolate themselves from the body of Christ. That's why it's essential for us to interact continuously with fellow Christians.

Purity Is Revealed by Our Thoughts

Health experts often proclaim, "You are what you eat," but a greater truth of eternal significance is summed up in the statement "You are what you think." Our ability to maintain purity depends greatly upon *where* our thoughts reside. Philippians 4:8 states, "Brethren, whatever is true, whatever is honorable, whatever is right, *whatever is pure*, whatever is lovely, whatever is of good repute, if there is any excellence and if anything worthy of praise, *dwell on these things*." William Gurnall, a

Puritan writer and pastor, wrote the following words about the effect our thoughts can have upon our conduct:

> Our hearts are of that color which our most constant thoughts dye into it. Transient fleeting thoughts, whether of one kind or another, do not alter the temper of the soul. Neither poison kills nor food nourishes, unless they stay in the body; nor does good or evil benefit or harm the mind unless they abide in it.[1]

Our hearts become what we dwell upon in our thoughts. Lustful, immoral thoughts that begin to dart about in our minds before we shoo them out the door of confession don't have time to take root. They don't linger long enough to affect our hearts to a great degree. It's only when we continue to dwell upon impure thoughts that our hearts become defiled, and that will go on to affect our words and actions.

Our garden of the mind sprouts weeds—daily! But that garden is easy to care for when we deal with the weeds while they are small and few in number. If we wait until the garden of our mind is choked by the weeds, then cleaning it becomes a monumental task. The same is true when it comes to dealing with tempting thoughts. For the good of our spiritual growth we can't afford to wait until our minds are overgrown with immoral and impure thoughts. When we become aware that we are thinking such thoughts, it's time to pluck weeds! If we truly desire to please the Lord and obey His command for purity, then we must keep watch over our thought life.

The Basics of Purity

You might find yourself thinking, *Perhaps I should skip the rest of the chapter. I don't have a problem with impurity or immorality.* But wait, don't skip ahead. Keep reading because the command to be pure contains application for everyone—no matter how old you are, how long you've known the Lord, or what your marital status.

God warns us to pay attention to His Word even if we don't think we need it: "Let him who thinks he stands take heed that he does not fall" (1 Corinthians 10:12). It's possible God may use some of the content in this chapter to reveal an area or two of impurity that may have crept into your heart unnoticed. So don't miss out on any opportunity to examine your heart and life for anything that may keep you from purity.

In Matthew 5:27-28, Jesus revealed there is a connection between sins of conduct and sins of the heart. So let's start there to identify any potential areas of impurity. When Jesus preached the Sermon on the Mount, He explained the various ways we are guilty of breaking God's law. For example, the law stated, "You shall not commit adultery" (verse 27), but Jesus gave further insight into God's mind when He explained, "But I say to you that everyone who looks at a woman with lust for her has already committed adultery with her in his heart" (Matthew 5:28).

Jesus was speaking to men here, but He could just as easily have addressed His comments to women. There is the temptation to excuse ourselves if we haven't committed the "big" sins of adultery or fornication, but Jesus' point is that adultery or fornication that remains hidden in the heart is still immorality. So instead of just focusing on our actions, we need to look for those sins of the heart that keep us from living purely before the Lord. Whether we find big sins or hidden ones, our initial response should be the same: confession and repentance, with a complete turning away from those sins.

Not one of us is free from sin. We are all guilty of impurity in some manner before the Lord. But we can overcome those temptations by clinging to the Lord and seeking to apply His commands. The guidelines that follow can aid us in making purity a priority.

True Believers Practice Purity

Did you know the continued practice of any kind of impurity is incompatible with a believer's calling? Ephesians 5:3-5 states, *"Immorality or any impurity or greed must not even be named among you*, as is proper among saints; and there must be no filthiness and silly talk, or coarse jesting, which are not fitting…no immoral or impure person… has an inheritance in the kingdom of Christ and God." A person whose life is characterized by continued patterns of impurity has no assurance of their salvation because their deeds declare they are of the world rather than of heaven. Notice that Ephesians 5:3-5 reveals *even minor degrees* of immorality and impurity should not be part of the godly person's life. That's because true saving faith is characterized by purity.

You Have the Power to Practice Purity

Remember, if you are born again, you are no longer a slave to sin. Christ's death cut the chains that previously bound you. You have been freed from sin's tyranny by faith in Jesus Christ, and you have received the grace to put those sins to death—if you are willing to kill them. Colossians 3:5 encourages you to have this mindset: "Consider the members of your earthly body as dead to immorality, impurity, passion, evil desire, and greed, which amounts to idolatry." If you are truly saved, you have the grace from God to put to death the deeds of the flesh (Galatians 5:24). Now that's great news!

Put Aside Fleshly Deeds to Practice Purity

The beginning steps for overcoming any entangling sin are found in James 1:14-15. James tells us that we give birth to sinful actions when our sinful thoughts have reached full-term. He says, "Each one is tempted when he is carried away and enticed by his own lust. Then when lust has conceived, it gives birth to sin; and when sin is accomplished, it brings forth death."

A heart steeped in the Word will take on the flavors of heaven rather than those of the world.

Then James goes on to say, "Therefore, putting aside all filthiness and all that remains of wickedness, in humility receive the word implanted, which is able to save your souls. But prove yourselves doers of the word, and not merely hearers who delude themselves" (James 1:21-22). When we put aside immorality and impurity and implant the Scriptures in our souls, the Word of God transforms our hearts and makes us like Christ. James urges us to act upon what we know is right rather than delude ourselves with make-ourselves-feel-better platitudes while remaining entangled in sin.

God's Word Helps You Practice Purity

Just like a cup of hot water becomes ambrosia because of the tea bag immersed in it, so a heart steeped in the Word will take on the flavors of heaven rather than those of the world. Psalm 119:9-11 has the answer for overcoming any and all sin: "How can a young man keep his way pure? By keeping it according to Your word. With all my heart I have sought You; do not let me wander from Your commandments. Your word I have treasured in my heart, that I may not sin against You." The Word of God is the key to growing in purity.

Obedience Helps You Practice Purity

God prizes quick obedience in His children. Parents are blessed when they see their children run to obey them. In the same way, God is blessed when we run to obey Him. The psalmist wrote in Psalm 119:60, "I hastened and did not delay to keep Your commandments." Quick obedience requires quick repentance and confession, which leads to increasing purity of heart and life.

Fleeing Immorality Helps You Practice Purity

You can tell purity is a priority to you when you *flee* immorality (1 Corinthians 6:18), *flee* youthful lusts (2 Timothy 2:22), and *flee* idolatry (1 Corinthians 10:14). The Greek word translated "flee" carries with it the idea of being a fugitive and running for your life. A classic example of fleeing immorality is the time when Joseph ran off when Potiphar's wife made sexual advances toward him (Genesis 39:7-12).

How would your life be different if you put this into practice every time you were tempted to immorality in some way? Now, after looking at the verses above, you might say, "I can understand why I need to flee immorality and youthful lusts in my battle for purity, but what does idolatry [1 Corinthians 10:14] have to do with purity?" That's a great question! Biblically speaking, to commit idolatry is to give to someone or something that which belongs to God. When our hearts are so taken by something that we focus on *it* to the exclusion or neglect of God, that's idolatry. Often it's our idolatry that leads to immorality and lustful passions. And we end up submitting to the idol of our flesh rather than God. That's why it's essential that we learn to flee immorality and the temptations to engage in immorality.

Special Focal Points of Purity for Women

Now that we have learned about purity and ways to maintain it, I want to spend the rest of the chapter focusing on four areas of purity that pertain to women specifically. Now whether you are a man or a woman, young or old, married or single, purity is purity. Yet as women, there are a few areas that we should concentrate on. These special focal points are centered on the fact that men are generally more susceptible to visual kinds of temptation, while women are generally more relationship oriented. Knowing that men and women are tempted in different ways helps us to better prepare for purity. Let's take a look our four special focal points of purity.

First, Focus on Pure Thoughts

Women often tend to overlook how their thought life can affect their purity. It may seem harmless to us to think about Mr. Darcy from *Pride and Prejudice* falling for us instead of Elizabeth Bennett, but this kind of daydreaming has its dangers. For the romanticizing and sexual thrills we may have received from imagining ourselves in his arms can progress from the *fictional* Mr. Darcy to the *real guy* in the next cubicle at our workplace.

And while there's nothing wrong with enjoying a romantic story, there is something wrong with thinking romantic or sexual thoughts about someone other than your spouse or who may be someone else's spouse. You may say, "But I'm not married and I'm not thinking about anyone who is married. So what's the problem?" The problem lies further down the road if that situation fits you. Getting married doesn't automatically shut off those kinds of flirtatious and romantic thought patterns we may have developed in our youth. Those thought patterns are habits, and habits are hard to break. Yet for purity's sake we need to consider our thoughts, daydreams, or fantasies: What are we really thinking about? And do those thoughts give glory to the Lord?

The command to be pure begins with our thought life. Affairs, both physical and emotional, began with *a* romantic thought—just one thought that leads to another one and another one. Before we may even realize it, we have committed adultery or fornication in our thoughts. Any one of us is susceptible to engaging in an emotional affair if we think about someone other than our own "Prince Charming." And we must *never* forget that every physical affair begins with romantic daydreams.

We are able to maintain purity in our thoughts when we are thankful and content with our situation and trusting the Lord to provide us with *our* Mr. Darcy, if it's His will.

God's priority for you is purity in your thought life.

Second, Focus on Pure Conduct

Just as wise men learn to guard their eyes from temptation, wise women too need to set up guards so they can maintain purity. We are at risk for emotional and physical affairs anytime we spend consistent, regular, or frequent time with men outside the relative safety of our homes. If you are married and work outside the home, then you must constantly remain on guard in your relationships with other men. Even if you are not married, and a "friendly" relationship with an unmarried man is acceptable, you must still learn to guard your thoughts and heart so you don't become emotionally attached to a person you may never marry.

Be aware of *what* you are thinking about other men, as well as *how often* you find your thoughts dwelling on a particular man, for those thoughts can influence your behavior. Godly men constantly take steps to guard their eyes so they won't fall into sexual sin, and we women, in like spirit, must do the same by guarding our conduct against anything that could lead down the road toward sexual immorality. For example, purity in our conduct is possible when we guard against flirting, guard against finding ways to build intimacy through conversations, and guard against touching or giving "friendly" hugs.

God's priority for you is purity in your conduct.

Third, Focus on Pure Speech

Are the things you talk about with your friends or family members characterized by purity? We learn from 1 Timothy 5:13 there are topics we should avoid in our conversations. We are not to "[talk] *about things not proper to mention.*" Ephesians 5:3-4 provides insight into what those things are: "*Immorality* or any *impurity* or *greed* must not even be named among you, as is proper among saints; and there must be *no filthiness and silly talk*, or *coarse jesting*, which are not fitting, but rather giving of thanks." The world loves to take part in such talk, but believers shouldn't engage in flippant or unholy conversation.

God's priority for you is purity in your speech.

Fourth, Focus on Pure Dress

THE CALL TO MODESTY

A man's battle for purity begins with his eyes, which is one of the reasons modesty is essential for every Christian woman. The sense of modesty and decorum that used to govern how a woman dressed has been replaced with a "flaunt it" mentality—even among Christian women. It's sad to say, but women often justify dressing immodestly. Many women also think this is a problem *other* women have, not themselves. And they believe the issue of immodesty is a man's problem, so they shouldn't have to change how they dress.

Yet no amount of mental gymnastics and wriggle-out-of-it rationalization can negate this one fact: God commands women to be modest. He tells us in 1 Timothy 2:9-10, "I want women to adorn themselves with proper clothing, modestly and discreetly, not with braided hair and gold or pearls or costly garments, but rather by means of good works, as is proper for women making a claim to godliness." God intends for any and every woman who claims to be a follower of Jesus Christ to dress modestly. That's just how it is—no ifs, ands, or buts about it.

Some may accuse me of being naive when I say this, but I believe *every* Christian woman knows if something she is wearing (or not wearing) is modest or not. I know I knew the difference, even as an unbeliever! A woman may try to quell her conscience through rationalizations, excuses, and blame-shifting, but those tactics don't fool God. He sees through the smoke screen of her excuses.

What God sees is pride, the root of all immodesty. Pride makes women want to flaunt their bodies. Pride delights in the power to tempt men, to attract attention to themselves and away from God. That is why Paul was so concerned about how women dress in church. Pride makes a woman unwilling to submit to God's calling to dress modestly. And that, dear ladies, is sin.

Modesty Basics

It is possible to dress both fashionably and modestly. Resources abound for any woman who wants to grow in purity through her modest attire. And the most easily accessible resources are other godly Christian women. Observe how some women *excel* at dressing modestly. Ask those women what criteria they use for choosing their clothing. You might also find it helpful to talk with your husband, father, or brothers about whether you need to dress more modestly and how to accomplish that task. You will discover that Christian men who desire to live pure lives have great advice about modesty. They are grateful when women make modesty a priority! A man who loves the Lord doesn't want to be distracted and tempted to impure thoughts by some provocatively or scantily clad woman, especially at church.

How can you determine if you are dressing modestly? Here are a few simple guidelines I have collected over the years that can help you no matter what your age, your season of life, or the occasion.

- A general rule of thumb is if you can see *up* it, *down* it, or *through* it, then it is not appropriate to wear in public.

- If it is so tight that people can tell what you look like without your clothes, then you shouldn't wear it.

- Remember the height factor. Generally men are taller than women, which means they look at you from a higher vantage point and may see more than you intend for them to see.

- Do a shrug test in front of a mirror to see how things look when you bend over or move your shoulders together.

- Make sure the bra you choose has enough padding to cover up your body "buttons."

- Skin is alluring to a man, which is why spaghetti-strap shirts or halter tops are a no-no unless paired with another covering of some kind. When asked about modesty, one young man responded, "Girls should show no more skin than the average guy." Now that's good advice!

God's priority for you is purity in your dress.

Be Pure Because He Is Pure

As we've discovered, God desires purity in thought, word, and deed for every woman. Understanding His expectation should motivate us—out of love for Him—to put away fleshly deeds, worldly desires, and lustful pride. The pernicious temptations of immorality and impurity can plague us with the same regularity as the ocean's tides, yet even though those temptations may continue to break over us like waves upon the seashore, we can get to a place of safety by leaning on the Lord.

We are called to purity because we are His children. And as such, we are to put off anything that may decrease our resemblance to our Father. Parents delight when they catch a glimpse of a little one emulating them in some way—how they sit or stand, or twiddle with a pen. I remember one time watching our youngest son morph into the likeness of a favorite uncle. One moment our son was walking down the street next to his uncle, and in the next moment there appeared to be two "Uncle Kevins" as our son mirrored the gait and posture of his uncle's distinct walk. That kind of eagle-eyed attention is exactly what every believer ought to have when it comes to imitating the character of God. The woman who desires to make purity her priority keeps her eyes fastened on her heavenly Father. And that delights the Lord! The apostle John wrote about this in 1 John 3:2-3:

> Beloved, now we are children of God, and it has not appeared as yet what we will be. We know that when He appears, we will be like Him, because we will see Him just as He is. And everyone who has this hope fixed on Him purifies himself, just as He is pure.

We know that someday we will be like our Savior, Jesus Christ. And it is that *someday*, that blessed someday, when we will see Him face to face that motivates us *now* to purify our hearts, to purify our minds, and to live pure lives because He is pure.

Now, that's a great motivation to be pure!

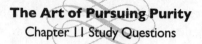

1. In what ways can others see purity in your life? See Proverbs 20:11; Luke 6:45; and Philippians 4:8.

2. Why should you remain pure? Look up Proverbs 5:21; 1 Thessalonians 4:7-8; and 1 Peter 1:14-16.

3. What standard of purity does God desire to see in our lives? See Ephesians 5:3-5; Colossians 3:5; and James 1:21-22.

4. How can a Christian remain pure? See Psalm 119:9-11,60; 2 Timothy 2:22; and 1 Peter 2:11.

5. A woman who makes purity a priority says no to what kinds of things? To what kinds of things will she say yes?

6. Are there any changes you need to make in your life so you can say yes to purity more often?

7. Many wonder, "Just how pure does a Christian need to be?" Because God is our standard for purity, we must align ourselves with what He desires for our lives rather than the standards of the world or our friends. What are some practical ways you can grow in purity according to God's standard?

8. Are there any obstacles that may stand in your way as you pursue purity? If so, what counsel does God's Word give you to overcoming those obstacles? What resources do you have for overcoming those obstacles (such as Scripture and other believers)?

Chapter 12

The Art of Caring for Your Home

When I was expecting our daughter Leah, I was still teaching public school. People asked me if I planned to go back to teaching after she was born. I'll never forget one man's reaction when I told him I intended to stay at home, take care of our children, and be a "worker at home." He predicted that in a couple years' time I would sit around, grow fat, read magazines, and talk on the phone all day. His cynical attitude made me wonder if that was what his wife had done.

In this chapter we come to one of the hot buttons many women struggle with—being a "homeworker." Misconceptions and misunderstandings abound on the topic, but balance and understanding can be achieved by taking time to look at exactly what God desires for women when it comes to being a homemaker.

In Titus 2:5 God says women are to be "workers at home." Apparently the idea of women working at home was a foreign one in Greek culture because Paul had to create a word that would precisely describe the focus and priority the home is to be. In popular English Bible translations, the compound Greek word has been translated as "homeworker," "workers at home," "busy at home," and "keepers of their own houses."

Today, many women work outside the home—some out of necessity, and some out of preference. If you are one of those working women, texts like Titus 2:5 may have made you feel a bit uncomfortable or guilty for working outside the home. You may have heard many opinions about the matter and wished for greater clarity on what the Bible says about this. So let me briefly say it's important to understand that God's priority for you is to tend to your home and all those who reside in it. But that doesn't mean you can't work outside the home too, for even within the Bible's pages we find some compelling examples of women who worked inside and outside the home. But you must consider two questions in light of this priority from God: *Why* are you working outside the home? And, Can you truly *fulfill* your responsibilities at home and to your family while also working outside the home?

There's no disputing the fact that God desires you to make your home and family a priority. And that can only happen when you are *at home*. Yet *how much* you need to be at home in order to fulfill your God-given priorities depends on you, what season of life you are in, the size of your family, the ages and needs of your children, and your husband's needs. What you *can* know with certainty is that you are to *work* at caring for the multitude of things related to your home and family!

A Homeworker's Focus

Contrary to popular propaganda, being a homeworker is more than merely keeping your house clean. As a worker-at-home you become like one of the chatelaines of a castle during medieval times. Those ladies-of-the-castle kept the estate in working order while their husbands were off doing battle with a neighboring earl, or hunting in some primeval wood. They oversaw the details of castle life and kept things running smoothly. In a similar way, you have been given the responsibility of taking care of and overseeing your castle as well as all the inhabitants who live within its walls.

That is why God entrusted a young woman's training in these important matters to the older women, for they have already learned the arts of homemaking. They are readily able to pass on to the younger women the goals, motivations, helpful tips, and survival techniques they have acquired over the years in keeping their homes to the glory of God.

What a Homeworker Is Not

If you are like me, you may find it helpful at times to learn what something is *not* in order to better discern what it *is*. The definition of being a "worker at home" becomes clearer from a look at what it isn't, so that's where we will start. As Paul gives instructions about how to care for the many widows in the early church, he also provides some guidelines for the young widows in 1 Timothy 5:13-15. His comments provide us with insight into the characteristics of a *non*-homeworker. The apostle Paul writes:

> At the same time they also learn to be idle, as they go around from house to house; and not merely idle, but also gossips and busybodies, talking about things not proper to mention. Therefore, I want younger widows to get married, bear children, keep house, and give the enemy no occasion for reproach; for some have already turned aside to follow Satan.

We learn from the above verses there is a connection between not caring for our homes and idleness. Paul even says some of the younger widows *learned* how to be idle. Though they hadn't previously been lazy, they became that way when the church stepped in to care for their needs after their husbands passed away. Without responsibilities, duties, or a husband to look after, they *learned* to become indolent.

We also discover from the verses above that the woman who neglects her home is often tempted to fill up her time by being a gossip and a busybody. With lots of free time on hand, boredom soon sets in, and with boredom comes the twin temptations of gossip and meddling. The woman who knows all the goings-on in the neighborhood is most likely not paying attention to her home or her children.

And regrettably that is the picture many people today have of a homeworker: An idle busybody who doesn't take care of her home or her family because she is so busy shopping, going to lunch, working out at the gym, and spending time everywhere but at home. I've seen this all too often. It's almost as if some women believe they are on a life-long sabbatical now that they are "at home." This is how the woman who is "at home" but not a "worker at home" opens herself up to temptation. Anytime we are in the wrong place at the wrong time doing the wrong things, we bring reproach upon Christ.

The fact that a woman is all too often away from her home and family reveals that her passions, desires, and priorities are not about caring for her home. This also sets her up for moral temptation and to become a temptress herself. Proverbs 7:11 says of this type of woman, "She is boisterous and rebellious, *her feet do not remain at home.*" She rebels against God's plan for her, doesn't take seriously the command to care for her husband and children, and acts as if being a stay-at-home mom gives her license to run around and play all day while her husband works. On the other hand, being a homeworker does not mean being barefoot and pregnant in the kitchen. It does mean watching over the home, to some degree, to earn the name *homeworker.*

Whatever the duties of a worker at home, they are certainly not like the "duties" of the gadabout woman we just looked at. We know for certain God desires His daughters to be diligent in all they do, to be productive, to contribute to the well-being of the family, to be sensible and pure in their conduct, to flee temptation, and to faithfully and joyfully fulfill their calling.

So what does God expect of us as keepers of the home? Surely there is more to it than merely keeping the floors and bathrooms clean.

P31 and You

It's time to call in the Bible's Homemaking Expert—P31.[1] Yes, that's it—the Proverbs 31 woman. Poor P31! Women react in funny ways whenever she's mentioned. They roll their eyes or smile sheepishly, and few really want to study her homeworker skills. P31 was the forerunner to the T2:3-5 woman. P31 exemplified the very qualities God desires to see cultivated in every Christian woman, so it's wise to spend some time looking at the actions and attitude a worker at home should possess.

Proverbs 31:10 asks, "An excellent wife, who can find?" which intimates it's difficult to find a truly excellent wife. The question implies that if a man does find an excellent wife he should hang on to her, "for her worth is far above jewels." More amazingly, P31's excellence increased over the years as she faithfully made her home and family a priority. Let's take a closer look at P31's example.

A Keeper of the Home Loves Her Husband

Proverbs 31:11-12 provides insight into the marriage of a keeper of the home: "The heart of her husband trusts in her, and he will have no lack of gain. She does him good and not evil all the days of her life." *A worker at home faithfully makes her husband a priority.* She continually looks for ways to do him good. Whatever he entrusts to her—his heart, the running of the home, the raising of the children, the finances—she seeks to guard and care for to the best of her ability. She works to build up the family and the home rather than tear them down.

Just like P31, you can show your husband he is a priority to you by doing something as simple as staying within your allotted budget when you go grocery shopping. When you manage the home in this way, "family meetings" can be a time of blessing and camaraderie rather than fear and failure. If your husband likes a clean and organized home, you can show he is your priority by keeping your home as he likes. Or your husband may prefer to show hospitality by having a constant influx of guests. If that's your situation, then you can show your husband he is your priority by becoming proficient at hosting people in your home.

What are some specific ways you can do good for your husband and build trust in your relationship in the way you oversee and care for your home?

A Keeper of the Home Has a Good Attitude About Work

P31 enjoyed taking care of her home. Proverbs 31:13 says, "She looks for wool and flax and works with her hands in delight." A home-worker enjoys caring for her home and taking care of the household—her attitude is one of *delight*.

A good attitude toward your work is a
demonstration of your love for God.

Work and delight may not happily coexist in your mind, but they can if you ask the Lord to help you. Think about it: If God wants you to be a worker at home, what kind of worker at home does He want you to be? Do you think avoidance, grumpy attitudes, or laziness are the best ways to respond to His priority for you? Even on days when you find it difficult to go the extra mile for your husband, it's always worth it to give 150 percent for the Lord. A good attitude toward your work is a demonstration of your love for God. Or think of it this way: What does a grumpy, reluctant attitude communicate to others about how you feel about God and His will for your life?

Taking care of your home—and all the "work" that goes with it— can become your joy and delight if you begin by asking the Lord to help you have a right attitude toward it. You can train yourself to think biblically about work by doing a study of what God says about it. No matter who lives in your house with you, it is still the Lord whom you serve (Colossians 3:24). *A worker at home has a good attitude about taking care of her home because she has a good attitude about obeying the Lord.*

What is your attitude toward the priority of being a worker at home? What steps can you take to develop or improve upon your attitude about being a worker at home?

A Keeper of the Home Is Enterprising

Not only does P31 work with her hands in delight, but she also "considers a field and buys it; from her earnings she plants a vineyard" (Proverbs 31:16). She actually searches for work! *She looks for ways to benefit the family and home with the skills she possesses.* She is enterprising and uses her skills—not to get herself out of the house, but to enhance her home. Her goal is to creatively look for ways she can bless her husband and her family.

P31 must have had an amazing amount of energy because verse 24 says, "She makes linen garments and sells them, and supplies belts to the tradesmen." Her industry in the home eventually extends to those outside the home, where she uses her skills to benefit others and make extra income for her family. She doesn't do this to the neglect of her family, but to bless them.

You may not have the energy or abilities of P31, but you can still creatively consider ways to bless your family. P31 used her energy outside the home to benefit her family, and this was *after* she had attended to the primary tasks of maintaining her own home. With everything running smoothly at home she then turned a portion of her attention to other endeavors, which allowed her to become an even greater blessing to her family.

What about you? What are some specific ways you can use your time and energy to bless and benefit your family?

A Keeper of the Home Feeds Her Family

A keeper of the home works to provide variety and interest in the family's meals. This doesn't mean every meal turns into a gourmet affair. Yet with a little forethought, preparation, and creativity, you can keep your meals from becoming ho-hum. Proverbs 31:14 reveals how P31 worked at this: "She is like merchant ships; she brings her food from afar." Merchant ships brought spices and food from other lands, and this woman would go hunting for unusual or hard-to-get foods so her family would have variety in their meals. You certainly don't need to go meet the cargo ships at the dock to secure some interesting new foods, but you could try a new recipe every now and then or introduce new healthy food items to your family. P31 kept her eye out for fresh, healthy, and delicious foods, and she prepared these foods to serve to her family.

Even if you are a disinterested cook, you can still work on your meal planning and preparation *for your family's sake.* I go through phases when I am more interested in cooking than at other times, but my husband and boys are always interested in food! For their sake I try to plan interesting and delicious meals for them to eat. What areas in your meal planning and food preparation could use improvement? How can you excel at this aspect of being a worker at home?

A Keeper of the Home Is Diligent

P31 showed diligence and purpose in caring for her home and family. Proverbs 31:15 states, "She rises also while it is still night and gives food to her household and portions to her maidens." You may groan at the thought, but P31 was so serious about fulfilling her divine calling that she was willing to sacrifice some precious early morning sleep.

A Proverbs 31 woman makes sacrifices to bless her family and honor the Lord.

A worker at home starts the day with a purpose and a plan, so she gets up early to get going on the day. She doesn't lounge in bed so long that when she does finally get up she is forced to run around like a chicken with her head cut off. She gets up to prepare and provide for the day's activities in the fruit of the Spirit. She prepares herself (shower, hair, makeup) and her heart (time in the Word and prayer) so she can better meet the needs of her family and home the rest of the day.

This brings us to one of P31's habits that, for some, causes concern, and that is her habit of rising "while it is still night." But that's not as bad as it sounds. P31 lived long before electric lights were invented, so it was dark *anytime* you got up before the sun came up. People went to bed when it got dark, and they got up when the sun came up. And in her efforts to watch over her household, P31 got up before everyone else.

How can you prepare for each day's events so you
meet them rather than collide with them?

I find that getting an early start on the day makes a huge difference in how I work at home. It was true when my kids were babies and toddlers, and it's still vitally important now that they are older. Getting up, spending time with the Lord, then getting ready, putting my face on, and brushing my teeth makes a significant difference in how I approach the day. When I have myself prepared, then I am better equipped to attend to the house and my family's needs with a cheerful and calm spirit rather than rushing about in a chaotic frenzy.

P31 also gave "portions to her maidens," which means she divvied up the day's tasks among her maids, who were on hand to help in the kitchen and care of the home. You may not have maids who can help you, but you can give your children tasks to do. As they work alongside you, you will be training them to take on responsibilities and develop life skills. We see that a Proverbs 31 woman has a plan and a purpose for what she wants to accomplish each day. How can you prepare for each day's events so you meet them rather than collide with them? What do you want to accomplish for your family and your home? A worker at home has a plan and a purpose.

One of the ways I worked at being purposeful at home was to write "house plans." When I was a public schoolteacher, I had to write lesson plans each week on what I intended to teach, and show how those plans met the goals of the class. After changing professions and becoming a worker at home, I was afraid I would forget about my priorities during the transition from schoolteacher to worker at home. In order to make sure I was purposeful with my days and had goals to aim for, I carried my lesson-plan habits into the home and wrote out my "house plans" for the week. It was good training for me to see how a little planning and preparation helped me to better attend to the goals and priorities of my home.

A Keeper of the Home Works Hard

There's no way around it—a worker at home works hard. Proverbs 31:17 says, "She girds herself with strength and makes her arms strong." *She grows strong from working hard at home*. If you are fulfilling God's calling for you, it will help you stay healthy and fit. It helped P31!

P31 worked hard even when others were ready for bed. Verse 18 states, "She senses that her gain is good; her lamp does not go out at night." She understands the worth of her work, and doesn't want to stop even in the evening. After she sets goals and deadlines for herself, she pushes herself to meet and accomplish them. Her attitude is to use each available moment for good. And when her lamp finally does go out at night, she sleeps well, knowing she has used her time wisely.

P31 was willing to work hard for the sake of her home and family. What about you? Are you willing to put forth the time and effort it takes to be a keeper of your home?

A Keeper of the Home Tackles the Hard Stuff

Proverbs 31:19 tells us, "She stretches out her hands to the distaff, and her hands grasp the spindle." Spinning wool and flax into cloth was a tedious job, but she didn't shirk that task. She even *reached out* her hands to it. It wasn't done grudgingly.

This reminds me of a friend who has a similar attitude when it comes to cleaning the bathrooms in her home. She tackles the bathrooms first before the rest of her housework to head off any fits of procrastination that might tempt her. I set a timer to help me work earnestly through the more tedious tasks instead of dawdling as I do them. Or, I use a phone headset when I call someone so I can keep my hands free to do work. For me, fellowship on the phone takes the tedium out of the dreaded chore. What kinds of jobs do you tend to put off for another day (or month)? How would your home be different if you went after those tasks with the diligence and cheerfulness of P31?

Oh dear—I need to go do some ironing!

A Keeper of the Home Is Prepared

A worker at home is prepared. It's evident she is prepared by the way she meets the needs of those outside her family. Proverbs 31:20 shows P31 at work: "She extends her hand to the poor, and she stretches out her hands to the needy." The Proverbs 31 woman desires to minister to the needs of others, which requires planning and preparation on her part. She is diligent in taking care of her family, and she also devises ways to help those in need who are within her sphere of influence. Something as simple as stocking up on the two-for-one sales at the grocery store allows you to share your extra supplies with someone who may have financial struggles.

Another way the Proverbs 31 woman shows foresight is by planning for her family's future needs. Proverbs 31:21 states, "She is not afraid of the snow for her household, for all her household are clothed with scarlet." P31 knew her kiddos would soon outgrow their tunics so she bought a goat, sheared it, washed and carded the wool, and…well, you get the picture. She thought about the long-term needs of her family.

We can follow P31's example by anticipating our family's upcoming needs. We can shop the clearance sales in the spring for the following winter's clothing needs. When we understand how quickly our children grow, we can budget for the shoes they will soon need. How do you plan ahead to meet the needs of your family and others who are in need?

A Keeper of the Home Pays Attention to Her Appearance

We have seen the many sacrifices the Proverbs 31 woman made on behalf of others. But what about herself? P31 not only took care of her family, but she also made sure she was appropriately dressed. Proverbs 31:22 states, "She makes coverings for herself; her clothing is fine linen and purple." Fine linen and purple were expensive materials in those days, which tells us she was nicely dressed. She didn't show up in her "wash-day robe" each time she went to the village well for water. She worked to keep herself presentable.

Following P31's lead in this area is a wise maneuver for all keepers of the home. Our appearance can reflect our attitudes about being a worker at home. Granted, there are days when we all look a little bedraggled, but with a little care and forethought we can at least leave home without wearing a stained T-shirt. After all, women who work outside the home usually have a certain dress code they must adhere to so that they are presentable. As a homeworker representative of God's priorities, it's wise to take a little time to consider your appearance. How are you doing in this area?

A Keeper of the Home Blesses Her Husband

P31 understood the effect her reputation could have upon her husband and family. Proverbs 31:23 states, "Her husband is known in the gates, when he sits among the elders of the land." A husband's reputation can be made or broken by the behavior, words, and appearance of his wife. This is why P31's husband so thankfully says of her, "Many daughters have done nobly, but you excel them all" (Proverbs 31:29).

Often when I meet new people, I notice that they talk about a husband in terms of his wife. They'll say things like, "That's Tom. His wife is so neat. She is a real go-getter, and their kids are great!" On the other hand, it's a reproach upon us if people say things like, "Oh, that's Tom. Poor guy. His wife is a bit of a trial to him, but he bears with it bravely."

We all have our quirks and kinks, which our dear Savior endeavors to straighten out if we let Him. But if we stubbornly cling to our idio-syncrasies—and dare I say sins?—then we bring reproach to our families and to Christ. *How you work in your home and care for your husband and children will be a blessing or a curse to them.* Will others count your husband blessed because he is married to you? If you are married, it is God's priority for you to work at blessing your husband.

The Fruit of Your Work

P31's diligence and hard work in caring for her home and family resulted in spiritual benefits as well. She wore strength and dignity, smiled at the future (verse 25), and spoke with wisdom and kindness (verse 26) as she devoted her heart to the Lord (verse 30). The fruit of her actions and the deeds of her life became a testimony of her godly choices.

Over the course of her lifetime, P31 devoted herself to the priorities and duties God gave her. She faithfully attended to the responsibilities God entrusted to her by caring for her home. And even if you don't have a home, or a husband, or children, you can still steadfastly practice the principles we have learned from P31. The goal for every woman, no matter what her circumstances, is to examine how she is attending to the specific priorities God has given *her*.

If you are faithful, then it will be said of you, as it was said of P31 in Proverbs 31:29-31, "Many daughters have done nobly, but you excel them all. Charm is deceitful and beauty is vain, but a woman who fears the LORD, she shall be praised. Give her the product of her hands, and let her works praise her in the gates."

W omen are to be workers at home—and for that, they need to be at home. How much a woman needs to remain at home in order to fulfill her priorities as stated in Titus 2:3-5 depends on the woman, her school or career status, the size of her family, the ages of her children, the needs of her husband, and so on. Whatever her situation, it is clear that she is to work at caring for her home.

1. Can you think of any reasons it is good for older women to train younger women to be workers at home? Read Titus 2:3-5 and 1 Timothy 5:13-14.

2. What is the connection between diligence and work? Remember, *diligent* means "industrious, hardworking, zealous, persevering, persistent, untiring, plodding, careful, thorough," and "patient." See Proverbs 10:4; 12:27; 2 Corinthians 8:22; 2 Thessalonians 3:10-12; and Hebrews 6:10-12 for help as you come up with your answer.

3. Now let's look at the opposite end of the spectrum—the sluggard! Look up the following verses and note the sluggard's actions, attitudes, and anything else you see: Proverbs 15:19; 18:9; 21:25; and 24:30-34.

4. How does God view a sluggardly person? What is His attitude toward those who work with diligence?

5. How does God want us to work as keepers of the home?

6. What are some results from our work? See 1 Corinthians 3:13-14; Colossians 1:10; and Hebrews 6:10.

7. What attitudes do you have toward your work at home? What areas do you need to put energy into so you are a diligent homeworker?

8. List some specific ways you can "look well to the ways of your household."

9. In what areas do you think you are doing well as a worker at home? In what areas are you weak? What are some steps you can take to strengthen your weak areas?

The Art of Showing Kindness

Joseph, the son of Bible patriarch Jacob, had been falsely accused of rape and thrown into prison. But God had not forgotten him. The Bible says, "The Lord was with Joseph and extended kindness to him, and gave him favor in the sight of the chief jailer" (Genesis 39:21). Not many details are given in the Bible about Joseph's time in prison, but it's reasonable to assume he was miserable. How Joseph needed the kindnesses extended to him by the chief jailer in that wretched prison! With indignity and shame heaped upon him, and his heart sore from being falsely accused, even the littlest kindnesses humbled and encouraged him. What was it that cheered Joseph? An extra scrap of bread perhaps? Clean straw to sleep on, or a kindly look from the normally gruff jailer? The Bible doesn't give us the specifics, but whatever it was, Joseph's spirit was cheered and revived by the kindnesses shown to him.

Kindness is a sweet balm that soothes our ruffled spirits and encourages and cheers our hearts. God Himself is kind and desires to see us show kindness to others, so much so that He made it a priority for us in Titus 2:5. Kindness is an attribute no Christian woman should be without, and no other quality will endear us to others like kindness! Let's learn all we can about it so we can put it into practice each day.

The Foundation for Kindness

Our ability to show kindness from the inside out begins with salvation and grows from there. Without the transforming work of the Holy Spirit in our lives, not one of us can *truly* exhibit godly kindness.

But even after being saved, day by day we must lean on the Lord and His strength, confessing sin and seeking to do what is right according to God's Word. As we seek to walk by the Spirit, His fruit will come forth in our lives—including *kindness* (Galatians 5:21-23).

God spoke to the nation of Israel through the prophet Micah, who posed this question to them in Micah 6:8: "What does the LORD require of you?" The answer? "To do justice, to love kindness, and to walk humbly with your God." Showing kindness is not optional. God expects us to be kind—and not in a grudging, halfhearted way, but with all the exuberance and commitment that comes from genuine love. To "love kindness" is a command for *all* believers, not just those with the gift of mercy. Anytime we love something we devote time and energy to it, and that is just what we are to do when it comes to being kind. God Himself *loves* kindness. Keep reading to discover a few ways He extends kindness to believers.

The Kindness of God in Salvation Toward Us

It was God's compassion and kindness for us that moved Him to send Jesus Christ to become the Savior of the world. The Scriptures attest to this in Titus 3:4-6:

> When the kindness of God our Savior and His love for mankind appeared, He saved us, not on the basis of deeds which we have done in righteousness, but according to His mercy, by the washing of regeneration and renewing by the Holy Spirit, whom He poured out upon us richly through Jesus Christ our Savior.

In those verses we see that God's great lovingkindness toward us moved Him to save us, though we had done nothing to deserve this mercy. He generously poured upon us kindness and mercy through the Holy Spirit. *God's kindness toward us was manifested in the gift of salvation.*

The Kindness of God's Will Toward Us

God's kind will toward us in salvation is seen in Ephesians 1:9, which states, "He made known to us the mystery of His will, according to His kind intention which He purposed in Him." God *intended* to do good for us ever since the Garden of Eden, when it was prophesied that someday there would come a Son of Eve who would crush the serpent. The great power and force of God's character and will is directed toward us to do us good in Christ. What a thought!

The Kindness of God in Heaven Toward Us

We can see another aspect of God's kindness to us in salvation in Ephesians 2:7, which states that God made us alive in Christ "so that in the ages to come He might show the surpassing riches of His grace in kindness toward us." Not content to stop at showing His kindness to us here on earth, God intends to drench us in grace when we are in heaven with Christ. Like many a dad who excitedly anticipates his children's delight when they receive a special gift, so God, in His kindness, planned the best surprise ever for His children—the glories of heaven!

> Everything God does is kind. Every one of His deeds
> is motivated and immersed in His kindness.

The Kindness of God's Ways Toward Us

It is God's nature to be kind. He cannot help but be kind to His children. Psalm 145:17 proclaims, "The LORD is righteous in all His ways and kind in *all* His deeds." Did you catch that? Everything God does is kind. Every one of His deeds is motivated and immersed in His kindness. *Huh? God acted kindly toward me when I lost my job, when my mother got cancer, and when my son started taking drugs? How can those things be kind?*

Situations like those *are* difficult trials, no doubt about it. But even in the trials we face, God intends to do us good. God desires to produce spiritual fruit in us through the difficulties He allows us to experience. Trials drive us to the Lord for comfort and strength. And as we take comfort in His presence, we experience many of His kindnesses to us.

Often we have no way of knowing how the particular situations we face could be an act of God's kindness toward us. But that's because we don't see the whole picture and God does. Because God is "kind in all His deeds," we can trust Him to do what is good and kind toward us. If you entrusted your soul to the Lord, you can entrust your circumstances to Him as well, for it is His love that moves Him to treat you kindly.

Your Motivation for Kindness

In fact, experiencing God's kindness should motivate us to live godly lives in every way. First Peter 2:1-3 states, "Putting aside all malice and all deceit and hypocrisy and envy and all slander, like newborn babies, long for the pure milk of the word, so that by it you may grow in respect to salvation, if you have tasted the kindness of the Lord." *Have you tasted God's kindness?* If you have been saved by grace and have been unconditionally forgiven of your sins, then the answer is yes. If you have enjoyed any blessings of earthly life, then you have feasted upon the many kindnesses of the Lord. Experiencing His kindness should motivate you to devour God's Word, to grow in holiness, and put away grumpy, selfish behavior.

Our ability and desire to show kindness to others comes back to the kindness and forgiveness we have received from God. When we understand the great debt we owe our Savior, then showing kindness to someone else seems a little thing in comparison. Jesus said of the woman who washed His feet with her tears, "For this reason I say to you, her sins, which are many, have been forgiven, for she loved much; but he who is forgiven little, loves little" (Luke 7:47). What we often fail to realize is no matter what our background and life situation, we have *all* been forgiven much—far more than we will ever need to forgive someone else.

One of the greatest motivations we have for showing kindness toward others comes from following Christ's example. Ephesians 4:32 states, "Be kind to one another, tender-hearted, forgiving each other, just as God in Christ also has forgiven you." Are you having trouble showing kindness to someone because you are harboring bitterness toward that person for some reason? No matter what is behind your inability to show kindness, you need to remember the great forgiveness you have received from the Lord. When you came to Him in salvation He forgave your sins, and even now extends forgiveness to you each and every day. He kindly receives you back every time you confess and repent of those sins that so easily entangle you.

There are times when we have been hurt by others to the point we don't want to forgive them. We would rather pray God's judgment down upon them—much like James and John wanted to command fire to come down out of heaven upon the Samaritans for rejecting Jesus (Luke 9:54). Rather than acting in such a rash manner, Jesus encouraged His followers in Luke 6:35 with these words: "Love your enemies, and do good, and lend, expecting nothing in return; and your reward will be great, and you will be sons of the Most High; *for He Himself is kind to ungrateful and evil men.*" God is kind to His enemies, and He wants His children to show kindness to their enemies. We are to follow His example. The Lord knows our circumstances, and He will help us show kindness beyond our natural ability if we will rely on Him for help.

Putting Kindness into Practice

And this takes us back to where we started, with the command in Titus 2:5 that we are to show kindness. Charles Spurgeon wrote eloquently about being kind:

> This is what you have got to wear, even on the outside—to put it on; not to have a latent kindness in your heart and a degree of humbleness deep down in your soul if you could get at it; but you are to put it on. It is to be the very dress you wear. These are the sacred vestments of your daily priesthood. Put them on.[1]

Acts 9:36 relates the story of a woman who *put on* the sacred vestments of kindness. The Bible says Dorcas "was abounding with deeds of kindness and charity which she continually did." Dorcas ministered to destitute widows by making them clothing, but it was her kindness that dressed their hearts (Acts 9:39).

First Timothy 5:10 lists practical ways the godly women of the early church *put on* the sacred vestments of kindness. They generously showed hospitality, humbly washed the dust and dirt from the feet of other believers, came alongside and helped those in distress, and gave themselves completely to "every good work." By looking for ways to minister to others, the compassion they felt in their hearts found expression in their deeds of kindness.

Be Kind in Your Deeds

Generally when we think of being kind we tend to think of actions or deeds to show kindness. *Kindness* is an action word. It compels us to do good for others in some way. It lifts us up out of our seats to meet their needs. Thinking of ways to serve someone is a perfect place to start when we desire to show kindness, but Scripture mentions other ways we can practice kindness. Let's look at four of them here.

Be Kind by Being Patient

Often when kindness is mentioned in the Bible, patience is nearby. That's the case in 1 Corinthians 13:4, where we read, "Love is *patient*, love is *kind* and is not jealous." That also happens in Galatians 5:22, where the apostle Paul lists the fruit of the spirit: "love, joy, peace, *patience, kindness*." Kindness is linked with patience the way cookies go with milk—you just can't have one without the other. We show kindness to others by being patient with them. When I think back upon the times I was impatient with my children, it makes me sad that I was unkind to them in this way. My impatience would show up as irritation or exasperation with their childish ways. Kindness is patient.

Be Kind by Living by the Golden Rule

First Peter 3:8 commands all of us to be *kindhearted* toward one another, which is another way of saying we need to be compassionate and loving. Colossians 3:12 similarly tells us to "put on a heart of compassion, kindness, humility, gentleness, and patience" in our interactions with one another. Don't you just love it when other people treat you this way? Hey! This is starting to sound like the Golden Rule: "Treat others the same way you want them to treat you" (Luke 6:31).

BE KIND BY GIVING AND RECEIVING REPROOF

Psalm 141:5 expresses the desire to be shown kindness in an unusual way: "Let the righteous smite me in kindness and reprove me; it is oil upon the head." *Reproving someone* is a bit like hitting someone over the head with a verbal two-by-four, yet there are times when, biblically speaking, it's one of the most loving things we can do for one another. When we show fellow believers an area of sin and help them to overcome it, we show them biblical kindness. We don't excuse their sin; rather, we seek to lovingly show them the error of their ways and turn them back to the right path (Titus 1:13).

BE KIND BY CONSIDERING ANOTHER'S CIRCUMSTANCES

We can show kindness to someone else by *considering the situation* they are facing. In a very practical way Job reminds us how we can minister to one another in Job 6:14: "For the despairing man there should be kindness from his friend; so that he does not forsake the fear of the Almighty." Those who are weak and hurting need special doses of kindness from their friends, yet often we are tempted to "help" them get better by ignoring or minimizing their sorrows, or telling them to "get over it." By compassionately remembering the challenging circumstances they are facing, and putting ourselves in their shoes, we are motivated to extend an extra measure of kindness to them.

We can live out the command to show kindness through our *actions* by showing patience toward others, living by the Golden Rule, giving reproof lovingly and humbly receiving it, and showing consideration for another's circumstances. Next, let's take a look at ways we can show kindness through our *speech*.

Be Kind in Your Words

Proverbs 31:26 says of the excellent wife, "She opens her mouth in wisdom, and the teaching of kindness is on her tongue." How would others characterize your speech? Would they say, "The teaching of kindness is on your tongue"? That's a tough one, isn't it? Words can spill out so easily, and often we don't even notice the impact they have on those who hear them.

We all know the difference a few kind words can make in our homes, with our friends, and among unbelievers. It is sad to say, but the family can often be the last place where kind words are spoken—even among believers. Though we might not be purposefully *unkind*, we still find ourselves not being *purposefully* kind with our speech either. God's Word teaches us how to show kindness in our speech, so let's take a look at some ways we can do that.

Be Kind by Guarding Your Lips

"Kindness speakers" choose their words rather than blurt them out. No wonder David prayed in Psalm 141:3, "Set a guard, O LORD, over my mouth; keep watch over the door of my lips." Kind speech begins by guarding what comes *out* of our mouths. But it doesn't stop there.

Airports have security scanners so no harmful things will pass through. The Lord provided a security scanner for our lips in Ephesians 4:29, which reads, "Let no unwholesome word proceed from your mouth, but only such a word as is good for edification according to the need of the moment, so that it will give grace to those who hear." By carefully screening out unwholesome words and allowing only edifying, gracious words to pass over your lips, you will become known as one who guards her lips.

Be Kind by Speaking Carefully

Proverbs 12:18 reminds us about the healing nature of kind words: "There is one who speaks rashly like the thrusts of a sword, but the tongue of the wise brings healing." Another proverb reminds us, "A soothing tongue is a tree of life, but perversion in it crushes the spirit" (Proverbs 15:4). Kind words bring healing to a jangled spirit. Think about those times when you spilled or broke something and the response was kindness rather than derision. What a blessing those gentle words were to your bruised feelings!

Kind deeds and kind words begin in
the heart with kind thoughts.

BE KIND BY SEEKING GOD'S WISDOM

Kindness speakers understand how words can give God glory and help maintain unity in our relationships. As we seek to guard our tongues and speak edifying words, we will quickly realize the necessity of asking God for wisdom regarding the best way to speak. Paul tells us, "Let your speech always be with grace, as though seasoned with salt, so that you will know how you should respond to each person" (Colossians 4:6). Our desire to respond graciously motivates us to use God's wisdom for our speech.

Kind deeds and kind words begin in the heart with kind thoughts. How we think determines how we act and how we speak, so it is vital that we prepare our minds to think kindly.

Be Kind in Your Thoughts

Some people seem naturally kind, while others have to work at overcoming their naturally acerbic nature. Yet even those believers who *seem* to come by kindness easily will tell you that it isn't always easy to remain kind on the inside. Many know the right things to do and say, but still struggle internally with unkind feelings and thoughts.

Generally, kind actions and kind words are precipitated by kind thoughts. I say *generally* because it's possible to act and speak kindly while inwardly struggling to maintain or even produce kind thoughts. However, we know that sowing a steady stream of critical thoughts will produce a harvest of impatience and malice. A heart devoid of kindness will reveal itself when innocent-sounding words are spoken impatiently. A strident tone reveals a deeper heart problem: kindness is missing.

The goal then is to figure out how to cultivate kind thoughts in our hearts. Hebrews 10:24 provides us with a hint: "Let us consider how to stimulate one another to love and good deeds." When we think long and hard about how to encourage and do good to one another, we will think kindly about each other. The act of thinking about ways to do good for others helps us to think about them with compassion and patience.

We can also learn to think kindly about others by remembering what we were like before the Lord drew us to Himself. Paul did this in Titus 3:1-3:

> Remind them to be subject to rulers, to authorities, to be obedient, to be ready for every good deed, to malign no one, to be peaceable, gentle, showing every consideration for all men. *For we also once were foolish ourselves*, disobedient, deceived, enslaved to various lusts and pleasures, spending our life in malice and envy, hateful, hating one another.

The act of remembering what we were like prior to our salvation levels our thoughts and keeps us from becoming critical and judgmental.

Anytime we find ourselves sloshing through the miry waters of unkindness we can mentally *sail* to Philippians 4:8 and wash our minds in its refreshing waters. Paul wrote, "Finally, brethren, whatever is true, whatever is honorable, whatever is right, whatever is pure, whatever is lovely, whatever is of good repute, if there is any excellence and if anything worthy of praise, dwell on these things." The stain from a sodden, critical, and grumpy spirit can be made clean if we choose to wash our thoughts with honorable, pure, and lovely thinking. And then our thoughts will take on the refreshing coolness of kindness!

Just like the floodwaters of Noah's time covered all the mountains, so kindness is to cover every area of our lives as well. We are called to minister to others with kind deeds or speak kind words or think kind thoughts about them—kindness is to pervade our lives.

Kindness and You

We've all known people who are exceptionally kind. It's a delight just to be near them! Yet it's God's desire that *every* believer be kind and a pleasure to fellowship with, not just the exceptional few. When you consider those who have shown you kindness, what attitudes, behaviors, and words mark them as kind? What do they do that encourages you the most? Taking a moment to consider what encourages you will help you pinpoint specific ways you can show kindness to others.

We cannot forget that our ability to show kindness originates from God. He poured out kindness in our salvation and continues to abundantly shower us with His loving-kindness each day. He has given every believer His Holy Spirit, who helps us to show kindness. We go to the Lord for help in every spiritual endeavor, and growing in kindness is no different. Ask the Lord for help. Study the kindness of God in the Bible. As you think on the many ways God has treated you with tenderhearted compassion, it will help you extend kindness to others. Look for opportunities to show kindness!

Charles Spurgeon compellingly urges us to show kindness to one another because it draws men's hearts to Jesus:

> If there is one virtue which most commends Christians, it is that of kindness; it is to love the people of God, to love the church, to love the word, to love all. But how many have we in our churches of crabtree Christians, who have mixed such a vast amount of vinegar and such; tremendous quantity of gall in their constitutions, that they can scarcely speak one good word to you...Imitate Christ in your loving spirits; speak kindly, act kindly, and do kindly, that men may say of you, "He has been with Jesus."[2]

Show kindness in your thoughts, words, and deeds. Show kindness in your homes, at church, and at work. Show kindness when you rise up in the morning and when you come to the end of your day. Show kindness because God is kind and has been so kind to you. Show kindness because it is a vital priority for every Christian woman. And when you do, others will say of you, "She has been with Jesus!"

The Art of Showing Kindness
Chapter 13 Study Questions

1. What do you learn about kindness from the following verses?
Look to see where kindness originates, what it does, and any
results that may come from it: Luke 6:27-36; Ephesians 2:4-
7; Titus 3:4-7; and 1 Peter 2:1-3.

2. We learn from God's Word that we must *choose* kindness
because it's not a natural attribute for us. Look up the
following verses and explain the choices we must make to
live out kindness: Micah 6:8; 1 Corinthians 13:4; Galatians
5:22-23; and Colossians 3:12.

3. Proverbs 31:26 says, "She opens her mouth in wisdom, and
the teaching of kindness is on her tongue." What kind of
teaching comes from your tongue? How's your kindness
quotient?

4. We've all known people who are exceptionally kind. What
attitudes, behaviors, and speech mark them as kind?

5. What attitudes do you need to possess so you can express kindness to others?

6. When do you most need kindness? When does your family?

7. Who can you show kindness to today or this week? Ask the Lord to help you pinpoint a practical way to show that person kindness.

8. Write out at least one verse that motivates you to show kindness.

Chapter 14

The Art of Loving Submission

You would think that after being married for a long time I would have this whole submission thing locked up tight and dealt with, but it's just not the case. Even after more than 25 years of marriage, I still struggle at times to submit to my husband—the husband I love, the husband I enjoy serving, the husband who has different ideas than I do about how things should be done—you know, that guy!

I am beginning to think women's struggles with submission may be our dirty little secret. In the same way men are reluctant to talk about how often they think lustful thoughts or sneak looks at immodestly dressed women, women rarely discuss how infrequently they submit to their husbands or how hard they fight against submitting before they finally "give in." It's rare to hear a woman admit she doesn't want to submit to her husband and often rebels against his leadership. I have heard women ask for prayer that they would become *more* submissive to their husbands or to have a good attitude about it, but it's not often I hear one forthrightly say, "I am not submitting to my husband."

Many women know and understand what the Bible teaches about submission, but there is often a gap between what they know and what they do. The dearth of male leadership in the church, home, and family is also an alarming trend. And while men need to step up to the plate and become the spiritual leaders God intends them to be, women must not use their husband's shortcomings as an excuse not to submit. Instead, women must accept responsibility for the role God has assigned to them and not become part of the problem. By refusing to submit, then by default women are leading, and if women are leading, then the men are…well, what are they doing? Not leading. Submitting to their wives? Oh dear, that is what plunged the human race into sin! Adam *followed* Eve. God's plan for the family and the church is for wives to submit to husbands. Now if the thought of submission alarms, scares, or makes you angry, then keep reading, for God's Word contains much that will comfort and encourage you as you seek to implement the final priority found in Titus 2:5.

The Challenges of Submitting

Submission can be a challenge for any one of us because it strikes at the heart of our own selfishness. Submission means we must willingly choose to give up our own plans or preferences and give way to our husband's leadership when it becomes a matter of his way versus our way. This is what makes submission difficult. Sometimes we want to do things our way, not our husband's way.

Our struggle with submission can be traced back to the Garden of Eden, where the issue of leadership was introduced. From the beginning, God had put Adam in charge. This is seen in several ways. Adam was created first (Genesis 2:7). Second, Eve was created from Adam, not Adam from Eve (Genesis 2:21-23). Third, Eve was created for Adam as a helper (Genesis 2:18). Fourth, Adam named Eve—Eve didn't name Adam (Genesis 3:20). All these things show Adam's headship over Eve before the Fall.

Especially noteworthy is the fact that after the Fall, Adam is held responsible for the fall of mankind, not Eve (Genesis 3:17). Why? Because Adam was the God-appointed leader. Plain and simple, Eve ate the fruit, and her husband *followed her* leadership. This is made clear in Genesis 3:17 when God dealt out the consequences of Adam's sin. He said, "Because you have listened to the voice of your wife, and have eaten from the tree about which I commanded you, saying, 'You shall not eat from it'; cursed is the ground because of you." By following Eve into sin, Adam both perverted God's role for himself and led the human race into sin.

One of the continuing consequences of Adam and Eve's sin is a woman's desire to lead. In Genesis 3:16, when God dealt out the consequences for Eve's sin, He said to her, "Your desire will be for your husband, and he will rule over you." Now desiring our husbands doesn't sound like a punishment, does it? Most would say it's good for a wife to desire her husband! So what are we missing?

> Through the cross of Jesus Christ men and women can experience the blessing God intended as both submit to His plan by fulfilling their proper roles.

It's best to understand Genesis 3:16 as saying, "Your desire will be for your husband's position as head, but he will rule over you." Now that fits with the context of the passage and explains what "desire" means! The grammar of the original Hebrew text indicates women would so strongly desire their husband's leadership position they would almost make themselves sick longing for it.[1] As a consequence for sin women would desire to be in control, but God called men to lead, and thus the agelong battle of the sexes ensued. Bible teacher John MacArthur wrote, "Sin has turned the harmonious system of God-ordained roles into distasteful struggles of self-will."[2]

Though sin contends against our God-given roles, the cross brings healing. Through the cross of Jesus Christ men and women can experience the blessing God intended as both submit to His plan by fulfilling their proper roles. A man's leadership and a woman's submission within the home, and within the church, does not need to be a "curse" and a source of constant friction.

Submission 101

It's a shame that the word *submission* inspires such fear and derision in many women, for the Lord intended a woman's submission to be a means of blessing to her, her home, the church, and the watching world. The word *submission* means "to arrange one's self under."[3] It's the *voluntary* attitude of giving in, cooperating, assuming responsibility, and carrying a burden. Biblical submission is a voluntary yielding of one's self to another's leadership.

Submission is often illustrated by the relationship between a person's neck and his head. Without the neck holding the head up and providing constant assistance, the head would be handicapped and unable to perform all the tasks it is called on to perform. This is a great illustration of the relationship between the roles God has designed for men and women. Women, the neck, support and encourage their husbands, the head, in their duties as leaders of the home.

When the neck is injured or can't do its job in some way, the result is pain. Other parts of the body try to compensate for the loss, and everything takes longer. It's not a good thing. An incorrect understanding of submission can be a pain in the neck, and that pain can travel to the head as well. This is why every woman must understand what God intends submission to look like, act like, and be like.

All too often the Bible is criticized for the way God designed men's and women's roles, as if God were a cosmic killjoy and His sole purpose in instituting submission was to give women a bad deal. Nothing could be further from the truth! God is no whistle-blowing lifeguard shouting, "All right! Everybody out of the pool," but an all-wise and loving Father who always does what is best for His children. The truth is that *everyone* submits at one time or another, and a wife's submission to her husband is only one part of a Christian's submission.

For example, in Luke 2:51 we read how Jesus submitted to His parents, while 1 Corinthians 16:16 exhorts us to willingly submit ourselves to the leaders in the church who labor with great diligence for our sake. In fact, each one of us is to subject ourselves to one another in the fear of Christ, according to Ephesians 5:21. Slaves were to be subject to their masters in everything (Titus 2:9), while young men are to submit themselves to the leaders in the church (1 Peter 5:5). And all of us are to subject ourselves to our heavenly Father, according to Hebrews 12:9. Not only that, but all believers are to yield to governing authorities (Romans 13:1, Titus 3:1). Think about it this way: When people are willing to submit to the police there is peace; when they refuse to submit there is chaos. Submission is one of the means God uses to bring about harmony in our relationships.

Ultimately, *everyone* submits. Everyone has to submit to someone else at some point—even Jesus did while He was here on earth. So when God's plan for women includes submission, it's not because He is singling women out and trying to be mean. Rather, He has a plan and a purpose for our lives that cannot be accomplished without submission. Imagine what would happen if everyone wanted to be a leader in the church and no one wanted to submit to anyone else! There would be bedlam. Yet when people willingly submit to qualified leadership, there is peace in the church (Hebrews 13:7,17). And in the same manner, when a wife submits to her husband's leadership, there is peace and harmony in the home.

The Parameters of Submission

Many women who fear submission don't realize biblical submission has well-defined guidelines that provide protection for women and help maintain unity in the church and home. By understanding when we should submit and when we shouldn't, we can eliminate much of the "bad press" surrounding submission. Virtually every text that addresses women's roles in the New Testament mentions submission, and several of them help us understand the parameters of submission.

When You Should Submit

Ephesians 5:22-24 states, "Wives, be subject to your own husbands, as to the Lord. For the husband is the head of the wife, as Christ also is the head of the church, He Himself being the Savior of the body. But as the church is subject to Christ, so also the wives ought to be to their husbands in everything." The foundations for biblical submission begin here, where we learn a wife is to submit to her *own* husband, just the one, not all men equally. Can you imagine what it would be like if women had to submit to *all* men? What a thought! Thankfully, God has protected women from such confusing and potentially frustrating circumstances.

We also learn from Ephesians 5:22-24 that a wife is to submit to her husband *just as* she would submit to the Lord Jesus. When a woman submits to her husband as she would to the Lord Jesus Christ, potential tensions and objections seem to disappear. I have to admit there have been times when I have had such a grumpy attitude about doing something for my husband that the only way I could get over it was to remember that when I submit to my husband, I am also submitting to Christ.

This is just like telling our kiddos, "When you obey Mommy, you're obeying God." Yet somehow it seems easier when we ask for this kind of obedience from our children, but this "transfer of submission" is essential for every believer to understand. Any act of obedience—or submission—rendered for another also becomes an act of obedience or submission rendered to the Lord. Sometimes understanding this truth is what helps get us over the hump so we can submit to our husbands willingly and cheerfully.

Ephesians 5:22-24 also teaches that the roles God created for men and women maintain order and harmony in the church and home. What a difference it makes when everyone knows what they should be doing—and does it. In our house, squabbles would sometimes break out if one of the kids tried to take on my role in an attempt to "be in charge" of the other two. Before long there would be mutiny and I would have to intervene as a referee. When wives allow their husbands to lead without a power struggle, then order and harmony reign in the home.

And finally, we learn from Ephesians 5:24 that wives are to submit to their husbands in *everything*. This is often the most difficult part of submission—the everything part. Surely God didn't mean everything, did He? Submit when you know the fastest way to the restaurant, but your husband knows another route—which he thinks is better—and wants to take that one? Submit when you have the afternoon planned, but he has a different way he wants to spend it? Submit when he decides you need to withdraw from a certain ministry because he feels you are getting too worn out? Yep, submit—in everything!

Lest I alarm you, let me assure you that submitting to your husband in everything doesn't mean you can't share your helpful ideas and insights. By all means, you can do that. But when he makes his decision, then it is time to submit. Some men delight in discussing all the pros and cons of a decision with their wives, while others quickly consult with their wives and then make their decision, and then still others rarely divulge what they are thinking until they announce their intentions. Whether you married a mull-it-over type of guy, or a make-it-snappy type of guy, or a decision-time-is-over type of guy, when *your guy* makes his decision about what is best for you and your family, then it's time for you to trust the Lord and willingly submit.

The building blocks found in Ephesians 5:22-24 form an essential foundation to our understanding of biblical submission, and we can add more layers of understanding with a look at 1 Peter chapter 3. Verses 1-2 tell us, "In the same way, you wives, be submissive to your own husbands so that even if any of them are disobedient to the word, they may be won without a word by the behavior of their wives, as they observe your chaste and respectful behavior."

Whatever Peter had to say about submission began with a reference point: "in the same way," which refers back to Christ's example of entrusting Himself to God while bearing up under sorrow and persecution (1 Peter 2:21-23). With Christ as an example of trust, hope, and a godly response, wives can learn to entrust themselves to the Lord even when they are living with an unbelieving or disobedient husband who may not treat them in a God-honoring way. Women in this situation are to engage in "silent preaching" through their godly and respectful behavior. Yet *all* women are to submit to their husbands, not only the ones married to disobedient or unbelieving husbands. And *every* woman's submission should be evident in her modest, pure, and respectful behavior, which comes from a gentle and quiet spirit.

First Peter 3:5 tells us submission was the way the holy women of olden times adorned themselves. These holy women beautified themselves by first putting their hope in the Lord, and not solely in their husbands. This is a key component of submission, and every woman who practices submission should entrust herself to God for His protection and His provision for her emotional, physical, and spiritual needs. The husband may be, and usually is, the human instrument through which God provides these necessities, but the godly woman still puts her trust in the Lord.

This is what Sarah did, according to 1 Peter 3:6. Sarah put her hope in God, not Abraham. You've heard of extreme sports? Well, Sarah introduced us to "extreme submission," which is why Peter cited her as an example. Sarah entrusted herself to the Lord even when she was afraid of submitting to Abraham's sometimes selfish and harebrained ideas.

First Peter 3:6 says we follow Sarah's godly example every time we entrust ourselves to the Lord's care when we submit to our husbands, rather than being crippled by fear and rebellion. Sarah is commendable because she trusted the Lord in some extreme situations, such as when Abraham, on two different occasions, told her to say she was his sister because he was afraid he would be killed and Sarah would be taken to become another man's wife! Thankfully, God delivered her on both occasions.

Sarah was put into a situation that few women find themselves. And she faced some difficult decisions: Should she have submitted to Abraham, saved her husband's life, and yet risked being taken as another man's wife in the process? Or should she have maintained her purity, refused to submit to Abraham, and exposed her husband's life to danger? As we observe Sarah's life, we must remember she didn't have the resources we have today. Sarah didn't even have the benefit of the law or the Ten Commandments to guide her, for she lived before they were given to the nation of Israel. By contrast, we have the complete teaching of God's Word on the subject of submission. Sarah submitted to her husband, but as she did so, she looked to the Lord in faith and hoped He would rescue her from her predicaments. And He did!

When You Shouldn't Submit

You may be shocked to learn the Bible actually tells a woman there are times when she shouldn't submit. For women that fact can—and does—make a world of difference in understanding and applying biblical submission. We find the exception to submission in Colossians 3:18, which states, "Wives, be subject to your husbands, as is fitting in the Lord." This verse tells us what we have learned before—wives are to submit to their husbands. But in this verse we learn a woman's submission has certain limitations. Submission can only be rendered to the degree that it is fitting and proper in the Lord.

Now that changes things, doesn't it? There are actually guidelines for submission! If your husband asks you to lie to his boss so he can play hooky and go fishing, you cannot submit to him. Why? Because the Bible tells believers not to lie (Colossians 3:9). If your husband wants you to look at pornography with him, you cannot submit to him because you would take part in immorality, which is a clear violation of Matthew 5:27-28. If your husband tells you not to attend church, you cannot submit to him. Why? Because it's wrong for you as a believer to be isolated from Christian fellowship and the teaching of God's Word when God tells believers to assemble together (Hebrews 10:24-25). When a woman is forced to choose between submitting to the Lord or her husband, she must choose the Lord. She cannot sin against God for her husband.

You can submit freely to any request that leads to whatever is pleasing and proper for a believer, but you cannot render submission in any situation that requires you to disobey or dishonor the Lord. God's Word and the pastors and leaders of your church can guide you and provide you with wise counsel when you aren't sure if you should submit to your husband or not.

Submission as an Offering

When we submit ourselves to our husband's leadership and entrust ourselves to God, we engage in a *voluntary* act of worship. Submission is not dependent upon another person's behavior, and when that is the case then submission becomes a voluntary act, an offering of love to our husbands and to the Lord. In essence, submission becomes a gift we give to our husbands not because they have earned it, but because we love and trust the Lord.

Yet even then there are times when you can find it downright difficult to give way to your husband's leadership. Thankfully, you can *prepare* your heart and mind for submission to your husband by reminding yourself that it is the Lord's command, not your husband's, that tells you to submit. Below are some practical ideas that will help pave the way for your heart to joyfully submit as you journey toward heaven:

- We can make sure we are regularly enjoying time in God's Word. The frequent reading and studying of the Bible will keep our minds and hearts in tune with the things that delight the Lord—one of which is submission.

- We can study and think about Christ's submission to His earthly parents and to His heavenly Father's will. He gave us an example to follow, so let's follow Him.

- We can pray about submission, asking the Lord to give us a willing and joyful attitude.

- We can remember it is our job to train and model for our children a biblical example of a wife's submission to her husband's leadership. What kind of an example are you providing for your kids?

- We can pray for our husbands, asking the Lord to give them wisdom, godly character, and clear direction as they lead our families.

- And most importantly we can remember Christ's humble submission to evil men and His willingness to submit to death on the cross for our sins.

This is not a perfect world, and husbands are not perfect people. You will have times when you will squirm under your husband's leadership, when you will vehemently disagree with his decisions and desire to grab the reins from him in frustration or fear. By entrusting yourself to the Lord during those times, you will find grace and the help you need to obey the Lord, and to lovingly, cheerfully, and gracefully submit to your husband.

Submission tests what we believe about God's sovereignty
and His ability to take care of us in *every* circumstance.

Entrusting Yourself to God in Your Submission

What about those times when your husband makes an unwise or even foolish decision that affects your family? A decision that may cause you to feel unprotected, vulnerable, and unwilling to trust your husband's leadership? Unless he desires you to sin or disobey God, you must still submit to him. It is at such times that the truth of God's sovereignty over all things becomes a supreme source of comfort and strength to a believer. God is not thwarted from His plan for you if your husband makes a poor decision. And any marital ups and downs you may experience as a result of unwise decisions can become tools of growth and good in the Lord's skillful hands (Jeremiah 29:11).

Submission tests what we believe about God's sovereignty and His ability to take care of us in *every* circumstance. You may find it scary to submit when your husband is an unbeliever, is not walking with the Lord, or has shown patterns of foolish decision making. You may even find it scary to submit when your husband is a godly man who desires to honor Christ in every way because he is a man who sees things differently than you do, and may have a different plan than you do for your future. When this happens, you must give your fears to the Lord and trust Him to work all things out for good (Romans 8:28).

When we trust the Lord in such situations, we become Sarah's daughters, who "do what is right without being frightened by any fear" (1 Peter 3:6). Sarah leads the way for every woman as an example of submission in trying and difficult circumstances. And we take on her likeness when we follow her example of turning from fear to faith in the Lord.

What kinds of fears about submission do we need to give up to the Lord? I'm sure we could come up with quite a list, but here are a few key ones for us to consider:

- Do we fear the consequences we might face if we submit to our disobedient or unbelieving husband?

- Do we fear that an unbelieving husband will never come to know the Lord?

- Do we fear always giving and not receiving, or fear being used, or not having our needs met?

- Do we fear that God doesn't know what He is talking about and think that our self-sacrificing submission will not make any difference?

These fears, and other similar ones, can choke our faith so that we fail to obey God by submitting. It can be tempting to give in to our fears and rationalize our way out of submitting to our husbands, yet this is not what God desires for us. The Scriptures tell us *our* responsibility is to submit to our husbands and, at the same time, place our hope in God. Our God is a mighty God, and nothing is too difficult for Him—even when it comes to working in our hearts to help us submit and in our husband's hearts to help them lead. God is faithful. He always takes care of His children, and we can trust Him to do what is right toward us.

The Purpose of Submission

I have to admit it; I'm a scaredy-cat. So often I have allowed my fears to steal the joy and adventure from life. And the priority of submission is sometimes a challenge for me—there are times when it's hard to trust the Lord and give Him my fears. Yet God never intended for submission to cause fear or misery for us women. God intended submission to serve as a means of blessing. And we do receive blessing when we obey the Lord and submit to our husbands.

Here then is the adventure! This is our chance to wrap our arms around this priority from God and make *His* priority *our* priority. For our response to this priority of submission determines the vitality of our walk with the Lord. If we are unwilling to obey the Lord in this way, we will become stunted, misshapen versions of the women God desires us to be. God loves us! He wants only what is best for us—and His best includes submission.

Every time we follow God's priority of submission we give Him glory. And that's what we live for, isn't it? To honor God with our lives? So let us lay aside our fears, our failures, and our faintheartedness...and trust that God will use this priority of submission to produce the fruit of trust, hope, and joy in our lives.

Now that's an adventure for a lifetime!

1. Biblical submission is the voluntary yielding of one's self to another's leadership in a number of our relationships, not only the husband and wife relationship. Look up the following verses and note who is submitting to whom in Luke 2:51; 10:17-20; Ephesians 5:21; Titus 2:9; 3:1; Hebrews 2:8; 12:9; and 1 Peter 5:5.

2. What are the conditions for when a wife is to submit to her husband? See Ephesians 5:22-24; Colossians 3:18; and 1 Peter 3:1-6 (read 1 Peter 2:13-25 first).

3. When shouldn't a wife submit to her husband, according to the verses above?

4. In your own words complete the following statements:

   I have learned submission is not...

   I have learned submission is...

God uses submission to…

The purpose of submission is to…

5. Based on what you've learned from these verses, is submission ever dependent upon another person's behavior? Why or why not?

6. What are some specific ways you can grow more gracious and willing in your submission to your husband?

Part 3

The Purpose of Following God's Priorities

Chapter 15

All to Give Him Glory

My husband had been copastoring a church in Idaho for nine years when the Lord moved us to a new ministry in California. As the news of our upcoming move became known to the congregation, we were amazed as people began to share how our ministry had affected their lives. What caught us by surprise was *the ways* our lives impacted others. "Thank you for just showing up to events at church." "I don't know if you remember, but when my dad died you called me and talked with me about the Lord and the comforts of heaven. Your phone call made such a difference." "Your passion for God's Word has changed how I study the Bible for myself." Simple things, little things, sometimes seemingly insignificant things left an imprint.

Their comments reinforced an important truth to us: *How we live matters.* What an encouragement this can be for all of us! For even as believers there are times when we feel our lives are small and insignificant. We may have times when we feel like no one really notices the details of our lives, the choices we make, or the convictions we live by. But people do notice—and so does God. And it is because people watch our lives that we are admonished in Titus 2:5 to live in such a way that the Word of God will not be dishonored.

On the night of His betrayal, Jesus prayed in the garden of Gethsemane, "I glorified You on the earth, having accomplished the work which You have given me to do" (John 17:4). To glorify God and do His work was the desire of Jesus' heart during His life, and the benediction at the end. We should live so that we can pray in a similar way:

"Lord, I seek to give You glory in every way while on this earth. I want to live each day with Your priorities as my priorities and accomplish the work You have given me to do."

The *work* God has given every woman to accomplish while here on earth is what we've been studying from Titus 2:3-5—our priorities from God. By diligently and faithfully pursuing God's calling, we can follow Jesus' example and bring glory to the Lord. With God's priorities as our focus, God's Word is not dishonored, but *honored*. That's the purpose of our lives as believers—to give God glory in all we say and do. Each priority is an opportunity to live our lives in such a way that we would not bring shame or reproach upon His Word. The reason older women are told to encourage the younger women is because we learn from one another how to obey the Lord with the result that "the Word of God will not be dishonored" (Titus 2:5).

> As you willingly live out God's priorities,
> your life brings honor to the Lord.

Each chapter of this book has examined one of God's priorities for women as found in Titus 2:3-5. As you willingly live out God's priorities, your life brings honor to the Lord. Look at the list below to see what happens when you apply God's priorities to your life!

- When you are reverent in your behavior, the Word of God will not be dishonored.

- When you are careful in your speech and refuse to engage in malicious gossip, the Word of God will not be reviled.

- When you aren't enslaved to much wine or anything else that may cause you to sin, but instead you exercise self-control over your flesh, the Word of God will not be maligned because of your behavior.

- When you teach others what is good, the Word of God will not be exposed to reproach.

- When you encourage and train other women to be sober-minded about their priorities, the Word of God will not be blasphemed.
- When you love your husband and your children, the Word of God will not be dishonored.
- When you are sensible and wise in your dealings, you won't bring reproach upon God's Word.
- When you are pure in every part of your life, evil things will not be spoken about God's Word.
- When you make your home a priority and oversee it with care, God's Word will not be exposed to reproach.
- When you show kindness in your speech and your life, the Word of God will not be dishonored.
- And finally, when you submit yourself to your husband, you will not bring reproach upon the Word of God.

What a privilege it is for you, as a believer, to honor the Lord through your life! Yet by the same token, Paul gently whispers a word of warning when he reminds us we need to make God's priorities our priorities so that "the word of God will not be dishonored." You can bring dishonor to the Lord if you choose to dismiss His Word and the priorities He has for you. Like leaving milk out on the table overnight, so the sin of disregarding God's Word causes a terrible stench of reproach upon God, His Word, and other believers. When women brush aside God's Word and fail to focus on His priorities, it can spoil God's reputation and ours as believers, and leave a bad taste in the mouths of unbelievers.

If a woman who professes to be a Christian gets entangled in sin, unbelievers will proclaim, "You Christians are such hypocrites. You talk about Jesus and your changed life, but I don't see any difference between your life and mine." And thus the name of God is derided and His Word blasphemed. Even other believers can be affected. Some may follow her poor example, while others may find their hearts disturbed and faith shaken when she brushes aside God's priorities.

There was a point when each of our kids, during the junior high years, seemed bent on embarrassing the family by doing odd things in public, like singing or dancing in the middle of a store, or doing some other unusual or attention-getting action. There were times when the other kids, with looks of horror on their faces, would appeal to me to make their sibling stop because people were going to think the rest of us were like that too! Most of the time I wasn't too concerned that the actions of one goofy junior higher would bring reproach on our family, but the embarrassed siblings definitely understood what God is communicating to us in Titus 2. The conduct of one person can either bring honor or dishonor upon the family.

God put His honor on the line when He called us to become His children and adopted us into His family. His reputation is at risk when we claim Him as our Father yet bring shame upon Him by not living according to His priorities. It's our job to represent the family of God in a positive way. It's because we represent Christ to the world that Paul ends his recital of God's priorities for women with an admonition and encouragement not to dishonor the Word of God.

John MacArthur comments on how our lives can bring reproach or honor to the Lord by saying:

> Paul's point is that not only the evil things we say and we do, but also the good things that we fail to say and do, dishonor God and His Word before the church and before the world. Unbelievers judge the genuineness and value of our faith more by our living than by our theology. In doing so, they judge the truth and power of the word of God by the way in which we live. The world judges the gospel, which is the heart of the word of God, by the character of the people who believe and claim to be transformed by it.[1]

Our lives should *look* different and *be* different because we *are* different. We are strangers and aliens in this world (1 Peter 2:11) and are to live with our eyes set on our true home—heaven (Colossians 3:1-4; 2 Corinthians 5:8-9). The Word of God attests that believers have been transferred from the kingdom of darkness to the kingdom of light

(Colossians 1:13), have been made into new creatures (2 Corinthians 5:17), have obtained a new heart (Ezekiel 36:26, and have received the Holy Spirit, who helps us to walk by the Spirit and not by the flesh each day (Galatians 5:16). Paul explained this total transformation this way: "I have been crucified with Christ; and it is no longer I who live, but Christ lives in me; and the life which I now live in the flesh I live by faith in the Son of God, who loved me and gave Himself up for me" (Galatians 2:20). Anyone who has experienced forgiveness through Jesus Christ is different! And that difference shows up in our changed hearts, minds, speech, conduct, and motivations.

It's been God's plan all along to use the transformed lives and hearts of every believer to witness to a watching world. Jesus explained this in Matthew 5:16 when He said, "Let your light shine before men in such a way that they may see your good works, and glorify your Father who is in heaven." All the qualities listed in Titus 2:3-5 are specific (and powerful!) ways you can let your "light shine" and draw attention to Jesus Christ.

Yet we can never live out these priorities in our own strength. We cannot represent any one of the priorities accurately unless we are leaning on the Lord and seeking Him through His Word. I say *represent accurately* because sometimes we are able to put on a good show in the flesh and yet not give glory to God, for without faith it is impossible to please God (Hebrews 11:6).

We have only this life during which we can live for Christ, strengthen other believers, and be a light to those in darkness.

We can never truly live out God's priorities if we don't go to the Lord for strength and grace every day. Titus 2:3-5 details God's priorities for every woman, but we should never get the idea we can accomplish these things as if we were merely checking items off our grocery list. We *do* these priorities out of gratitude for our Savior. We *do* these priorities because we have been made into new creatures in Jesus Christ. We *do* these priorities because the idea of dishonoring the

Lord is repugnant to us. And we *do* these priorities because we love Him and desire to keep His commandments. There is no drudgery, no doldrums in making God's priorities our focus because He is the reason for everything we do.

We have only this life during which we can live for Christ, strengthen other believers, and be a light to those in darkness. Knowing God prizes the priorities of Titus 2:3-5 in every woman's life makes it simple for us. We know what God's will is for us. We understand how important it is to Him, and have learned some of what it means to put His priorities into practice in our lives. Let us look eagerly "for the blessed hope and the appearing of the glory of our great God and Savior, Christ Jesus; who gave Himself for us to redeem us from every lawless deed, and to purify for Himself a people for His own possession, zealous for good deeds" (Titus 2:13-14).

We are His daughters. Let's give ourselves to His priorities—for His sake, that the Word of God may not be dishonored.

> In full and glad surrender we give ourselves to Thee,
> Thine utterly, and only, and evermore to be!
> O Son of God, who lov'st us, we will be Thine alone,
> Our being and possessions, shall henceforth be Thine own![2]

1. According to Titus 2:5 and verses 11-14, what is God's plan for bringing glory to His name?

2. What are some potential pitfalls of God's method? What's the remedy?

3. Compare whose honor is at stake in Titus 2:5 versus Titus 2:8. How does that information help you focus on God's priorities even more?

4. On the night He was betrayed, Jesus prayed, "I glorified You on the earth, having accomplished the work which You have given Me to do" (John 17:4). Jesus' desire was to glorify God in everything He did, and we should have that desire as well. The work God has given you to do is summed up in the priorities of Titus 2:3-5. To what degree have you seen yourself make progress in accomplishing these priorities as you've read your way through this book? What one or two priorities are you especially excited about cultivating more?

5. Do you see any potential trouble spots you want to take care of so you can continue to honor the Lord? What are some specific ways you can strengthen those weak areas?

6. Write a prayer to the Lord declaring your commitment to adhere to the priorities and principles of Titus 2:3-5.

Notes

An Invitation to Discovering God's Best for You

1. Mary D. James, "All for Jesus," *The Celebration Hymnal* (Nashville: Word Music/Integrity Music, 1997), p. 588.

Chapter 1—God's Unchanging Priorities for You

1. John MacArthur Jr., *The MacArthur New Testament Commentary: Titus* (Chicago: Moody Press, 1996), p. 1.

Chapter 2—*The* Mindset for Every Woman

1. James Strong, *The Exhaustive Concordance of the Bible* (Nashville: Thomas Nelson Publishers, 1996), s.v. "encourage."

2. W.E. Vine, *Vine's Expository Dictionary of Biblical Words* (Nashville: Thomas Nelson Publishers, 1984), s.v. "sober-minded."

3. Our family uses Logos Bible study software. It's an excellent tool for any student of the Bible, and there are also some great online Bible study helps. You can try http://www.esvstudybible.org/online, http://net.bible.org/home.php, or http://www.biblegateway.com/ to get started.

Chapter 3—From Youth to Maturity

1. Dwight L. Moody, http://www.thewordteaches.com/QuotesJQ.htm.

Chapter 4—The Art of Growing in Holiness

1. Read more about Esther's story in the book of Esther in the Old Testament. The scene in which she appears before the king is found in Esther 4:9–5:8.

2. *Random House Webster's College Dictionary* (New York: Random House, 1999), s.v. "behavior."

3. Charles H. Spurgeon, *Evening by Evening,* ed. Alistair Begg (Wheaton, IL: Crossway Books, 2007), December 11, p. 361.

4. Spurgeon, *Flashes of Thought* (London: Passmore & Alabaster, 1888) p. 205, as cited in Steve Miller, *C.H. Spurgeon on Spiritual Leadership* (Chicago: Moody Publishers, 2003), p. 72.

Chapter 5—The Art of Speaking Pleasant Words

1. James Strong, *The Exhaustive Concordance of the Bible* (Nashville: Thomas Nelson Publishers, 1996), s.v. "malicious gossips."

Chapter 6—The Art of Self-control

1. James Strong, *The Exhaustive Concordance of the Bible* (Nashville: Thomas Nelson Publishers, 1996), s.v. "enslaved."

2. John Kirk, *The Mother of the Wesleys: a Biography* (Edinburgh: Rallantyne and Co., 1864), p. 145.

3. Thomas Watson, *The Godly Man's Picture* (1666; repr., Carlisle, PA: The Banner of Truth Trust, 1992), pp. 151-52.

4. Ibid., p. 148.

Chapter 7—The Art of Sharing and Seeking Wisdom

1. A.T. Robertson, *Word Pictures in the New Testament* (1932-33; Oak Harbor: Logos Research Systems, 1997), Titus 2:3.

2. The most comprehensive resource on men's and women's roles, biblical answers to feminism, and gender issues is The Council on Biblical Manhood & Womanhood website at www.cbmw.org, which has articles, links, books, and audio messages addressing virtually every issue imaginable on the subject. The site has a search engine that enables you to find the resources that will help you the most.

3. George Burch, *Nuggets of Gold: 2001 Spurgeon Quotes* (Greenville, SC: Ambassador-Emerald, 1999), p. 156.

Chapter 8—The Art of Loving Your Husband

1. Matthew Henry, *Matthew Henry's Commentary on the Whole Bible: Complete and Unabridged in One Volume,* electronic ed. (Peabody, MA: Hendrickson, 1996), John 21:15.

Chapter 9—The Art of Loving Your Children

1. J.C. Ryle, *Duties to Parents* (1888; repr., Choteau, MT: Old Paths Gospel Press), pp. 36-37.

Chapter 10—The Art of Living Sensibly

1. William D. Longstaff, "Take Time to Be Holy," *The Celebration Hymnal* (Nashville: Word Music/Integrity Music, 1997), p. 656.

Chapter 11—The Art of Pursuing Purity

1. William Gurnall, *The Christian in Complete Armour* (London: Thomas Tegg and Son, Printers, 1837), p. 612.

Chapter 12—The Art of Caring for Your Home

1. My friend Logan Carr coined this name for the Proverbs 31 woman and graciously gave me permission to use it in this book.

Chapter 13—The Art of Showing Kindness

1. Charles H. Spurgeon, *A Collection of Sermons*, index created by Christian Classics Foundation, electronic ed., Logos Library Systems (Simpsonville SC: Christian Classics Foundation, 1996), p. 192.

2. Charles H. Spurgeon, "Christ's People—Imitators of Him" No. 21, *Spurgeon's Sermons: Volume 1*, electronic ed., Logos Library System (Albany, OR: Ages Software, 1998).

Chapter 14—The Art of Loving Submission

1. Carl Friedrich Keil and Franz Delitzsch, *Commentary on the Old Testament* (Peabody, MA: Hendrickson, 2002), 1:64 on Genesis 3:16.

2. John MacArthur Jr., *The MacArthur Study Bible*, electronic ed. (Nashville: Word, 1997), Genesis 3:16.

3. James Strong, *The Exhaustive Concordance of the Bible* (Nashville: Thomas Nelson Publishers, 1996), s.v. "submission."

Chapter 15—All to Give Him Glory

1. John MacArthur Jr., *The MacArthur New Testament Commentary: Titus* (Chicago: Moody Press, 1996), p. 88.

2. Francis Ridley Havergal, "From Glory unto Glory," http://wordwisehymns.com/2009/12/23/today-in-1873-from-glory-to-glory-written.

Lisa and her husband, Jack, live in Southern California, where Jack is the teaching pastor of the church they attend. As the wife of a devoted and busy pastor, Lisa's ministry involvement has ranged from serving in the nursery to planning church picnics, and her greatest joy has been to write and teach Bible studies for the ladies in her church. It is her desire to see women develop a hunger for God's Word and watch as the Lord transforms their lives through the study of the Scriptures. You can learn more about Lisa's ministry by visiting her website at www.lisahughes.org or by going to http://afirmfoundationministries.com. You can also write to her in care of Harvest House Publishers, at:

Lisa Hughes
c/o Harvest House Publishers
990 Owen Loop North
Eugene, OR 97402

Other Great Harvest House Books

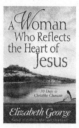

A Woman Who Reflects the Heart of Jesus

Elizabeth George

There is much we can learn from Jesus' perfect life example. Every woman who desires to reflect His character will find a treasure trove of truths and applications that enable her to follow Him well.

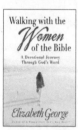

Walking with the Women of the Bible

Elizabeth George

From Eve to Esther, from Rahab to Priscilla, you'll find that women of the Bible were people like you. As you explore their stories, you'll find sparkling gems of God's love, truth, and wisdom at work in their lives and discover just how much God cares for you.

Women Counseling Women

Elyse Fitzpatrick, general editor

This rich and practical counseling resource looks to the Bible alone for God's perfect counsel to women who struggle with negative habits and addictions, emotions such as anger and depression, various kinds of loneliness, and more.

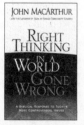

Right Thinking in a World Gone Wrong

John MacArthur, general editor

Today's media has a powerful influence on the way people think. How can we know what to believe, or not believe? This book will equip believers with scriptural guidelines for viewing today's controversies and concerns through God's eyes.